eat * sleep * shop

AMSTERDAM
STYLE GUIDE

MONIQUE VAN DEN HEUVEL

MURDOCH BOOKS
SYDNEY · LONDON

DROPS
ON A
LOTUS
LEAF

APPELHOENTJE
ERS GEGRILDE KIPFILET. LE PUY LINZ
ASTINAAK, RAMMENAS & CASHEW

BOER ZOEKT WORS
OOKWORST, BOERENKOOL. ZUURKOOL E
EBAKKEN UITJES. MET HUISGEMAA

SJAKIE EN DE BONE
MENGDE BONEN, PADDENSTOELENM
BAKKEN SPEKBLOKJES. MET YOGH

CONTENTS

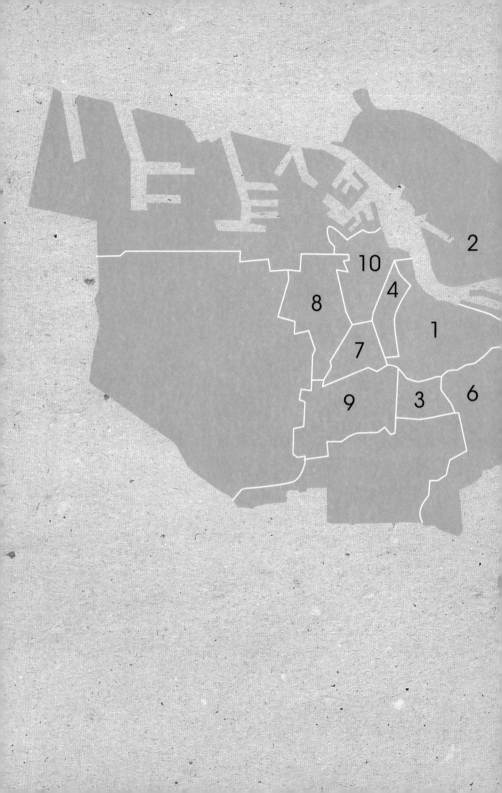

11

5

AMSTERDAM

WELCOME TO
AMSTERDAM

I love wandering around this city; slowly sauntering or cycling along the canals, through narrow alleyways, past picturesque 'hofjes' (courtyards) and squares. Not choosing the well-travelled path, but finding my own way, taking turns and seeking hidden beauty, often finding it in the unexpected.

I have been living in Amsterdam for the past twenty years and I still enjoy the city immensely. In this book, I want to share with you the spots that make me smile, those gems you might not otherwise find. Rather than focus on large museums and famous restaurants, I'll help you find small shops down little side streets; cosy markets in old factory halls with stalls selling handmade regional products; and coffee bars serving really great cappuccinos. These are the type of places where you're likely to find yourself chatting to a local, or chilling in a lazy hammock on a terrace. Amsterdam has enchanting old theatres and lunch spots so breathtakingly beautiful in their design they have to be seen to be believed. ✿

The Indische Buurt, De Baarsjes and Bos en Lommer are neighbourhoods brimming with creativity and innovation while Amsterdam Noord, across the River IJ to the north, where the city's shipyard used to be, has a raw and industrial feel to it. Old factory buildings are interspersed with quiet city beaches and the odd East German vintage store.

I love shops and hangouts that are a little quirky and managed with love. Places where you can spend time talking to the owner and feel welcome and at home, where the products have been carefully selected or handmade by local designers, with respect for people and the environment. Where the food is healthy, organic and vegetarian. Places that are surprising and doing something new, or simply old-fashioned but of amazing quality. Amsterdam has so many of these wonderful places, just waiting to be discovered.

In writing this book, I hope to show you a side of Amsterdam you wouldn't have found so easily otherwise. Please, join me and relish the city as much as I do.

Enjoy!
Monique

You can follow me on Instagram @moniquevdheuvel for even more Amsterdam inspiration.

MY 24-HOUR MUST DO'S

If you asked me to create an itinerary for the perfect day in Amsterdam using the places mentioned in this book, here's what it would look like:

I would kick things off with a latte and a croissant at neighbourhood gem **RUM BABA** (page 172) in Transvaalbuurt. While there, I would check my phone to find out where the moveable feast **HET BAKBLIK** (page 178) was located that day, then I'd head there and buy a few lavender cakes for the road. After that, I'd cycle to the **FLEVOPARK** (page 156) for an envigorating morning hike while enjoying the beautiful rhododendron blooms.

After all that walking, I'd have worked up an appetite for hummus from the Israeli brothers at **SIR HUMMUS** (page 104), they make everything from scratch using a secret recipe.

The afternoon is for shopping. My first stop would be **ALL THE LUCK IN THE WORLD** (page 98) to buy a handmade piece of art. As I like finding inspiration in the unknown, I'd take a ferry across the IJ to visit the design studio of **VLINDER & VOGEL** (page 58) where I'd pick a pretty postcard adorned with dried, pressed flowers. I'd continue my bike ride, crisscrossing the raw and industrial neighborhood of Noord, to **BLOM & BLOM** (page 83) to stare in awe at vintage design from the former German Democratic Republic (GDR). Then I'd relax on one of the boat benches at **CAFÉ DE CEUVEL** (page 86), a fully sustainable chill-out venue on the waterfront.

In the evening, I'd opt for an authentic Italian pasta served at **KOEVOET** (page 128) where the décor looks just like it did a hundred years ago, followed by a theatre performance at the tiny **ROODE BIOSCOOP** (page 22). On Wednesdays, traditional neighbourhood songs from De Jordaan are sung here. My night would end at **HOTEL DROOG** (page 34), a design department store turned hotel with just the one room on their top floor.

SHOPPING

1 I LOVE VINTAGE
2 SUKHA
5 &KLEVERING
6 RESTORED
10 ANNA + NINA
15 1027
16 LOCALS
18 LIKE STATIONERY
19 LAURA DOLS
21 J.C. HERMAN
22 THE OTHERIST
23 MARIE STELLA MARIS
26 HAAR BARBAAR
28 VLINDER & VOGEL

EATING & DRINKING

3 VINNIES
7 MEDITERRANE
8 KOKO COFFEE & DESIGN
12 BAKHUYS
13 METROPOLITAN
14 CENTRA
17 VAN STAPELE
20 DR. BLEND
24 VEGABOND
27 AMSTERDAM ROEST
29 INSTOCK
30 BACK TO BLACK

SLEEPING

11 HOTEL DROOG

CULTURE

4 ROODE BIOSCOOP
25 DE UITKIJK

MARKETS

9 BOERENMARKT

NOORD
HET IJ
ROZENGRACHT
DAM
NIEUW MARKT
LEIDSESTRAAT
LEIDSE PLEIN
VIJZELSTRAAT

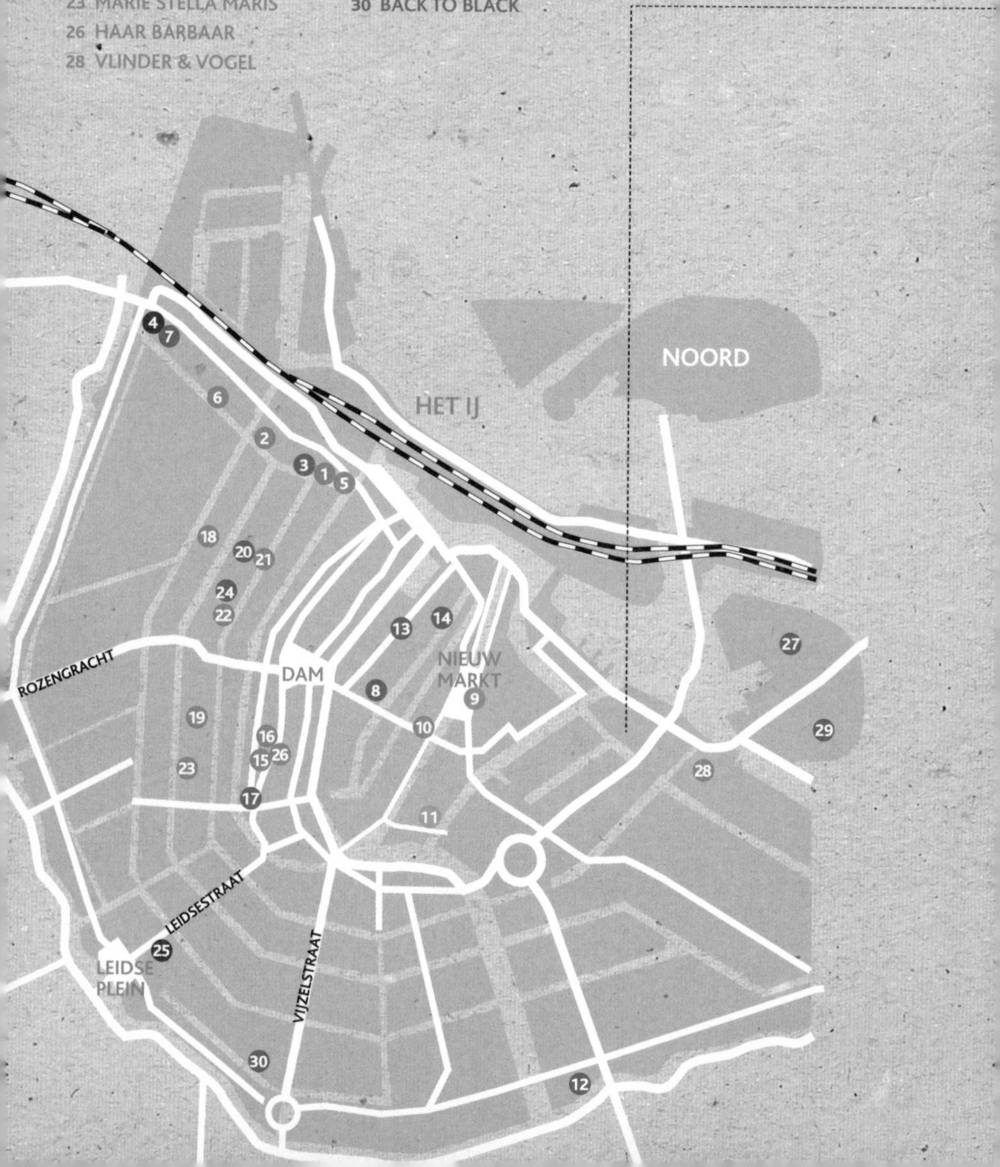

CITY CENTRE

Amsterdam's city centre is perfect for taking long walks, and even better for exploring the canals in a little boat. To escape the busy streets full of chain stores and the long museum queues, you'll have to veer off the beaten track. Locals tend to avoid the typical tourist areas. Rather than follow the canals, choose a perpendicular path that crisscrosses side alleys and leads from one canal to the next. That way, you'll stand a much better chance of finding the hidden gems tucked away around streets like Haarlemmerstraat, Utrechtsestraat, and squares such as Spui and Waterlooplein.

1. I LOVE VINTAGE

Do you adore vintage and retro clothes from the roaring twenties, fifties or sixties, but prefer them unworn? Well this shop sells 'new vintage' – brand new, but retro-style clothes. They stock beautiful brands such as Bettie Page, Hell Bunny and their own sustainable label Bannou, designed by owner Faranak. The only products that are truly vintage are their one-of-a-kind boots and bags. They have a great online shop, but nosing around their store makes me much happier.

Haarlemmerstraat 25,
Prinsengracht 201, 1015 DT Amsterdam
020 3301950
www.ilovevintage.nl

IRENE MERTENS

Stepping into **Sukha**, the concept store of stylist **IRENE MERTENS**, is to submerge yourself in beauty. It's no wonder this shop is namechecked in so many international home and design magazines. Sukha (which means 'joy of life' in Sanskrit) sells clothes, crockery and home accessories from brands that are kind to people and animals. They also stock handbags, often handmade, by Dutch designers. You'll recognise the shop by its window of whimsical illustrations and handwritten notes. These same illustrations and notes are printed on their free postcards, and appear on many Pinterest boards.

2. SUKHA
Haarlemmerstraat 110, 1013 EW Amsterdam, 020 3304001
www.sukha-amsterdam.nl

SUKHA AMSTE

'Amsterdam is always buzzing, but you can seek out some peace and quiet if that's what you feel like.'

HOW WOULD YOU DESCRIBE THE 'AMSTERDAM STYLE'?

It's a city that's always buzzing, but you can seek out some peace and quiet if that's what you feel like. There's no true 'Amsterdam style' but if there were, I would describe it as nice and loose.

WHAT'S IN YOUR SECRET ADDRESS BOOK?

The Westerpark for lovely walks and of course the Haarlemmerstraat for shopping. I also like Amsterdam Noord, an up-and-coming area with new places opening all the time. For food and a spot of sunshine, I go to Pllek. On Sundays, I like strolling around the many pop-up galleries.

WHERE DO YOU GO TO FIND INSPIRATION?

I find inspiration by walking the streets of the city. Amsterdam architecture is wonderful and each neighbourhood has its own charm. I also love sitting outside on a terrace and watching the world go by.

WHAT'S YOUR FAVOURITE AREA?

The area around Westerpark and the Houthavens. That's where new initiatives come to life. There's lots of building work being done, bringing new things and ideas.

WHAT'S STILL ON YOUR TO-DO LIST?

I really have to visit De Hallen (restaurant). It's time I finally saw and tasted for myself what everyone has been talking about all this time. Also, I'd like to visit all the pop-up stores that have been opening up recently.

WHAT IS ABSOLUTELY NOT TO BE MISSED IN AMSTERDAM?

Rent a bike and discover the city that way. Or take the ferry to Noord, have lunch at Eye and go see a movie while you're there.

Thuis.
De drukke buien buiten
daar zit ik nu niet mee
ik ga gewoon naar binnen
bij mezelf op de thee

Sukha

3. VINNIES

One of the first organic lunch joints in the
city, and a perfect spot for foodies. In this little
corner shop on the Haarlemmerstraat, Vincent
and Jules make the most delicious organic
coffee (from Bocca), sandwiches and salads.
Find a seat among the many pieces of vintage
furniture, art and keepsakes, all of which are
for sale. Like your restaraunts even cosier?
Stroll along to their other Vinnies location in
the old city centre.

Haarlemmerstraat 46, 1013 ES Amsterdam
020 7713086
Nieuwezijds Kolk 33, 1012 PV Amsterdam
020 2332899
www.vinnieshomepage.com

4. ROODE BIOSCOOP

Stepping into this tiny Art Deco-style theatre is like stepping back in time a hundred years. As the name suggests ('roode bioscoop' means 'red cinema'), back then it was a cinema showing mainly socialist propaganda films. These days you can sit, surrounded by dark red walls, and enjoy a line up of musical theatre, jazz and improvisations from around the world, chansons and poetry you aren't likely to hear anywhere else. On the last Wednesday of every month, there's a special show dedicated to the atmospheric songs and ballads of the De Jordaan area.

Haarlemmerplein 7, 1013 HP Amsterdam
020 6257500
www.roodebioscoop.nl

5. &KLEVERING

At the top of Haarlemmerstraat you'll find one of two &klevering shops, selling beautiful tableware, bags, cushions, lamps and quirky vases shaped like animals. I like going there to look at their lovely (cook)books – no one in town does a prettier display. Besides their own brand, &k, they also sell products from well-known labels including Normann Copenhagen and HAY.

Haarlemmerstraat 8, 1013 ER Amsterdam
020 4222708
Jacob Obrechtstraat 19A, 1071 KD Amsterdam
020 6703623
www.klevering.nl

25

6. RESTORED

This shop, on the busy Haarlemmerdijk, sells nothing but unique and original products by young designers: clothes, jewellery, ceramics and bags, and beautifully designed magazines and books. Nearly everything is handmade and every product comes with its own story. The owners are interested in the beauty of products. Have a good look around, because the interior and styling of the shop alone are worth the visit.

Haarlemmerdijk 39, 1013 KA Amsterdam
020 3376473
www.restored.nl

7. MEDITERRANE

When I visit the Haarlemmerbuurt
neighbourhood, I always make time to stop
at Mohammed's place, Mediterrane, where
the amazing smells of homemade bread and
pastries fill the air. The croissants, pain au
chocolats and frangipane tarts are the best
outside Paris. The shop itself would have
been perfect as a location for the film *Amélie*.
It's always lively and busy, filled with locals
having a cappuccino and a pastry. Don't
be put off by the long queue on Saturday
mornings – this one's worth the wait.

**Haarlemmerdijk 184, 1013 JK Amsterdam
020 6203550**

8. KOKO COFFEE & DESIGN

Karlijn and Caroline opened their coffee and design store right in the middle of the red light district, occupying the ground floor of an old canalside house. They were inspired by the many concept stores they encountered in London and Copenhagen, and they both love vintage, which is clear when you see the interior design of KOKO. You can either get comfy with a latte on the second-hand leather sofa, or browse clothes, home accessories and art by Scandinavian brands such as HOPE and Libertine Libertine. Set aside some time to check out the ever-changing collection of art by young talent.

Oudezijds Achterburgwal 145, 1012 DG Amsterdam
020 6264208
www.ilovekoko.com

9. BOERENMARKT

Every Saturday, in the shadow of the historical Waag building (once one of the city's gates), the Nieuwmarkt hosts a proper 'boerenmarkt' (farmers' market). Wander between stalls selling organic fruit and veg, bread, wines and natural cosmetics. The market isn't huge, but it's all the cosier for it, and it provides a meeting place for the locals that inhabit the area surrounding the Nieuwmarkt and the red-light district.

Nieuwmarkt, 1011 MA Amsterdam

10. ANNA + NINA

Enter Anna + Nina and you can't help but feel like you've turned into Alice in Wonderland as you stare at all the weird and wonderful things around you. Owners Anna and Nina travel the world searching for extraordinary jewellery, paintings, cushions, clothes, botanical products and vintage cupboards. There's nothing two-of-a-kind here, only products produced on a very small scale. The owners also run an equally beautiful shop of the same name in De Pijp.

Kloveniersburgwal 44, 1012 CW Amsterdam
020 2611767
Gerard Doustraat 94, 1072 VX Amsterdam
020 2044532
www.anna-nina.nl

11. HOTEL DROOG

This hotel has only one room, so it's really more a place for eating, drinking, shopping and enjoying art than a hotel. The owners of celebrated design label Droog Design built this extraordinary oasis with a magical garden in the middle of the city centre. Enter their fairytale world with flowers and (edible) plants everywhere. But are they real?

Staalstraat 7B, 1011 JJ Amsterdam
020 2170100
www.hoteldroog.com

12. BAKHUYS

In the middle of this bakery you'll find a large wood-burning stone oven. In the morning, it's used to bake seemingly non-stop batches of artisanal bread, cookies and pies. The fire crackles and pops while you sip your latte or eat your croissant, and the aroma of freshly baked bread fills the air. Owner Henk uses the same traditional recipes his father and grandfather used. Bakhuys' interior is lovely, with robust lamps and long wooden tables.

**Sarphatistraat 61, 1018 EX Amsterdam
020 3704861
www.bakhuys-amsterdam.nl**

Desem Pizza's
Tre Formagg
Spicey Pumpk
Tonno
Parma
Vega
Farmer
Pizza Bakhu

13. METROPOLITAN

Are you a fan of dark chocolate? Chocolatier Kees Raat makes the most delicious chocolates and homemade ice cream in his shop in the busy De Wallen area (Red Light District). He's the author of several bestselling cookbooks and was one of the first chocolatiers to use pepper in his chocolate. All of his products are made with the finest organic ingredients. You can attend one of the chocolate-making workshops in his work studio in De Jordaan, where he will reveal his secrets and give you recipes to take home.

Warmoesstraat 135, 1012 JB Amsterdam
020 3301955
www.metropolitandeli.nl

14. CENTRA

Lovers of paella find each other in this typical Spanish restaurant in a small alleyway in the De Wallen area (Red Light District). The interior hasn't changed in twenty years and it's a place where people meet and greet each other enthusiastically. The fresh fish on display can make an appearance on your plate in fifteen minutes, if you so desire – everything is super fresh and super fast here. Centra doesn't take reservations, but don't let that stop you because you won't have to wait too long.

Lange Niezel 29, 1012 GS Amsterdam
020 6223050
www.restaurantcentra.nl

15. 1027

In a tiny alleyway, Taco and his friends opened a wonderful place to have a haircut and meet new mates. The owner is a celebrated hairdresser who once worked behind the scenes of major fashion shows for the likes of Gaultier and Kenzo. His shop is kitted out with vintage furniture, the record player crackles in the background and the walls are covered in art. There's only one mirror and the customer chairs face each other, so chatting comes easily. You've no choice but to trust your hairdresser when it comes to your 'do. Pop in at the end of the afternoon, when the place fills with people, young and old, the wine bottle is opened and the music is turned up.

Raamsteeg 2, 1012 VZ Amsterdam
020 4226796
www.10-27.com

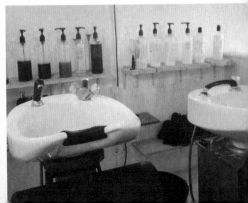

16. LOCALS

Filled with pretty scarves, bags, jewellery and crockery, all made by Dutch designers, this shop is a must-visit. Owner Suzanne is a jewellery designer herself and likes to showcase all the wonderful things her fellow Dutch designers are producing. She also stocks her own brand, Sugarz Jewelry. All products at Locals have a special story or are handmade.

Spuistraat 272, 1012 VW Amsterdam
020 5286500
www.localsamsterdam.com

17. VAN STAPELE

Owner Vera experimented for months, trying out hundreds of recipes, in search of the perfect chocolate cookie. Her friends were so delighted by the results, they convinced her to start selling them. Now, Vera bakes her crunchy chocolate cookies with molten white chocolate inside and sells them from her tiny, lopsided shop where time appears to have stood still (check out the sturdy wooden counter and the large chandeliers). Judging by the queue of locals and tourists, you'd think she was giving away her wares for free. A fresh sheet of cookies is pulled from the oven every ten minutes, so you won't have to wait long.

Heisteeg 4, 1012 WC Amsterdam
06 54241497
www.vanstapele.com

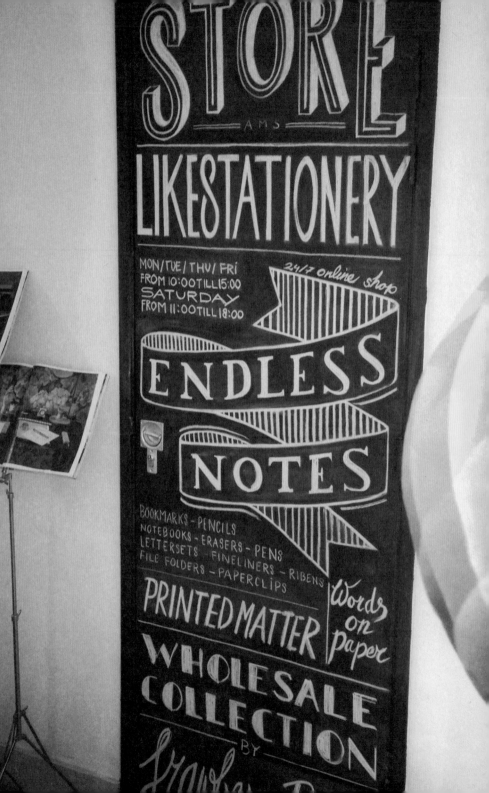

18. LIKE STATIONERY

Graphic designer Sanne sells the prettiest handmade notebooks, botanical print postcards and writing gear. The shop doubles as a design studio, where she works, in-between serving customers, on creating designs for magazines, books and fabrics. Sanne is a true paper lover and it shows. Ask away, she'll happily tell you all she knows about stationery.

**Prinsenstraat 24, 1015 DD Amsterdam
06 14359266
www.likestationery.com**

19. LAURA DOLS

If you like fifties vintage, don't miss Laura Dols. This thrift store is known throughout Amsterdam and has been located in the famous Negen Straatjes (meaning 'nine streets') for thirty years. It sells the most gorgeous evening dresses, bags, shoes, hats and jewellery. The owner travels the world looking for vintage finds, regularly replenishing her stock with new treasures. It's no surprise the shop regularly features in fashion magazines like *Vogue* and *Elle*. Don't skip the basement, it's filled with second-hand eveningwear.

**Wolvenstraat 7, 1016 EM Amsterdam
020 6249066
www.lauradols.nl**

20. DR. BLEND

This is where the locals come to pick up a healthy morning smoothie on their way to work. Owner Jamahl is not only a health nut, he's also a morning person, so you'll most likely find him behind the counter himself. Dr Blend sells delicious smoothies, salads and wraps — all organic. I recommend the Mango Django with pineapple, mango and turmeric. Right at the back, there's a wall full of superfoods and vitamins for sale.

Herenstraat 23, 1015 BZ Amsterdam
06 47964686
www.drblend.nl

21. J.C. HERMAN

Handmade vases, plates, bowls and lots of beautiful tableware – this ceramic artist's shop has it all. Potter Herman Verhagen throws all his own creations on a pottery wheel at the back of his shop. There are pieces everywhere, drying on shelves to be finished later. It's a place where locals put in special orders for weddings and birthdays.

Herenstraat 10, 1015 CA Amsterdam
06 57945494
www.jcherman.org

22. THE OTHERIST

This small canalside shop is a treasure trove of curiosities and vintage finds. Owners Joshua and Steven are usually the ones behind the counter and they love talking to customers about their amazing butterfly and insect collections, and their porcelain animal skulls. They also sell pretty painted crockery, handmade bags and unique jewellery. They search the world over for additions to their collection of rarities – making this the perfect address for purchasing an extraordinary gift.

Leliegracht 6, 1015 DE Amsterdam
020 3200420
www.otherist.com

23. MARIE STELLA MARIS

The Marie Stella Maris concept store is a joy to behold, thanks to its mostly white interior. It sells natural mineral water, supporting clean drinking water projects around the world, and also stocks a wide range of organic skincare products and cosmetics that use ingredients such as coconut oil and lemongrass. Tucked away in the basement is a cosy Parisian café that serves a breakfast of latte and a croissant.

Keizersgracht 357, 1016 EJ Amsterdam
085 2732845
www.marie-stella-maris.com

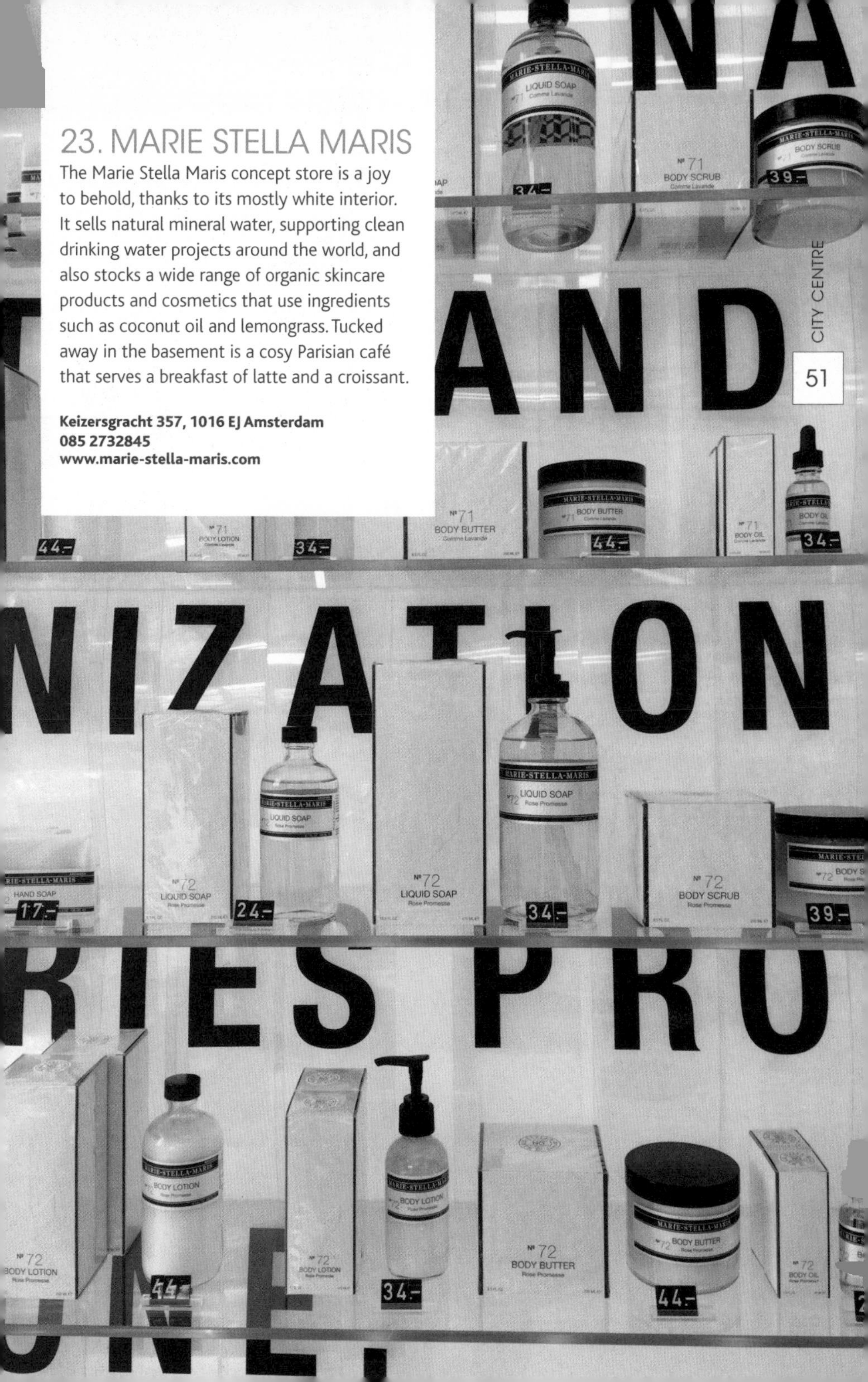

24. VEGABOND

This lunch spot/shop is a vegetarian's nirvana. Owner Babet and her sister create the best tempeh wraps, green smoothies and organic juices. Many of the products they sell are vegan and gluten-free, too. The large windows make it a great place to sit and watch the Amsterdam canal life go by. Don't forget to stockpile some of the goodies from the shop before you go. I recommend the handmade raw chocolates and the energy balls!

Leliegracht 16, 1015 DE Amsterdam
020 8468927
www.vegabond.nl

25. DE UITKIJK

This tiny cinema has eighty seats (plus a balcony) and it used to only serve the city's elite. It's the oldest movie theatre in the Netherlands and worth a visit for the stylish 1920s foyer alone. The cinema is now run by film-loving students and is the place to go to for quality films. No blockbusters I'm afraid.

Prinsengracht 452, 1017 KE Amsterdam
020 2232416
www.uitkijk.nl

26. HAAR BARBAAR

This barber shop is for men only, as is clearly stated in the shop window. It's fully kitted out, in rockabilly American style, with sturdy vintage chairs and stuffed animals. Men with large tattoos and names like Donnie, Joey and Nick trim and close-shave the beards of the city's creative types. They don't take appointments, but watching them at work is part of the experience and makes it worth the wait.

Rosmarijnsteeg 4, 1012 RP Amsterdam
020 4317683
Wolvenstraat 35, 1016 EN Amsterdam
020 7737175
www.haarbarbaar.nl

27. AMSTERDAM ROEST

Located in the former Koud Gas Gebouw (meaning 'cold gas building'), on the industrial Oostenburg Island, is the creative city oasis that is Roest. A minimal amount of work has been done to make this a cultural space for all, and an underground feel still lingers. Veg out on one of the chesterfields and grab your own drink from the fridge. On hot days, it seems the whole city comes to laze on the neighbouring city beach, where you can lounge in a deckchair with your toes in the sand. On weekends, they organise exhibitions or theatre shows – or there'll be a DJ playing or a vintage market in one of the adjacent halls.

Jacob Bontiusplaats, 1018 PL Amsterdam
020 3080283
www.amsterdamroest.nl

28. VLINDER & VOGEL

Spatial designer Saskia de Valk runs her own design studio where she likes to work with flowers. She creates gorgeous miniatures of dried and pressed flowers and branches that she finds outdoors, and enhances them with needle and thread. She makes small print runs of these, and sells postcards, too. Her work is regularly featured in well-known magazines. I recommend signing up for her workshops, which will teach you how to make your own creations using flowers.

Nieuwevaart 3, 1018 AA Amsterdam
06 18229112
www.vlinderenvogel.com

29. INSTOCK

After working for a large supermarket chain, colleagues Merel, Selma, Freke and Bart were disturbed to see how much food was being thrown out simply because it had reached its sell-by date. Together, they opened a restaurant that serves delicious food *and* raises awareness about food waste. Their team of creative chefs use 'past their best' products collected from that same supermarket chain to create a breakfast, lunch and three-course dinner every day. They also run a takeaway shop on Ferdinand Bolstraat 88.

Czaar Peterstraat 21, 1018 NW Amsterdam
06 49712261
www.instock.nl

1/3

WERELDWIJD
WORDT JAARLIJKS
1/3 VAN ONS
VOEDSEL VERSPILD

VERLIES VAN HULPBRONNEN

De oogst van 28.940 km2 kan bespaard worden met 40% mindervoedselverspilling in Europa

Dat is 3/4 van Nederland

30. BACK TO BLACK

This cute café, in a former living room, with its tiny terrace and turquoise gate feels just like a cosy home. They make a really good cup of coffee and the organic pastries are homemade. The cosy coffee bar is crammed full of plants, art and things for sale – you can even buy the tables and chairs. These kinds of places always make me happy as they are so relaxed and personal. Everything has been designed by Dutch designers, which is a plus, too.

Weteringstraat 48, 1017 SP Amsterdam
06 11194870
www.backtoblackcoffee.nl

KLAPROZENWEG

HET IJ

A10

7

4
5
6

11

8

3 1

2

VAN DER PEKSTR.

9

CENTRUM

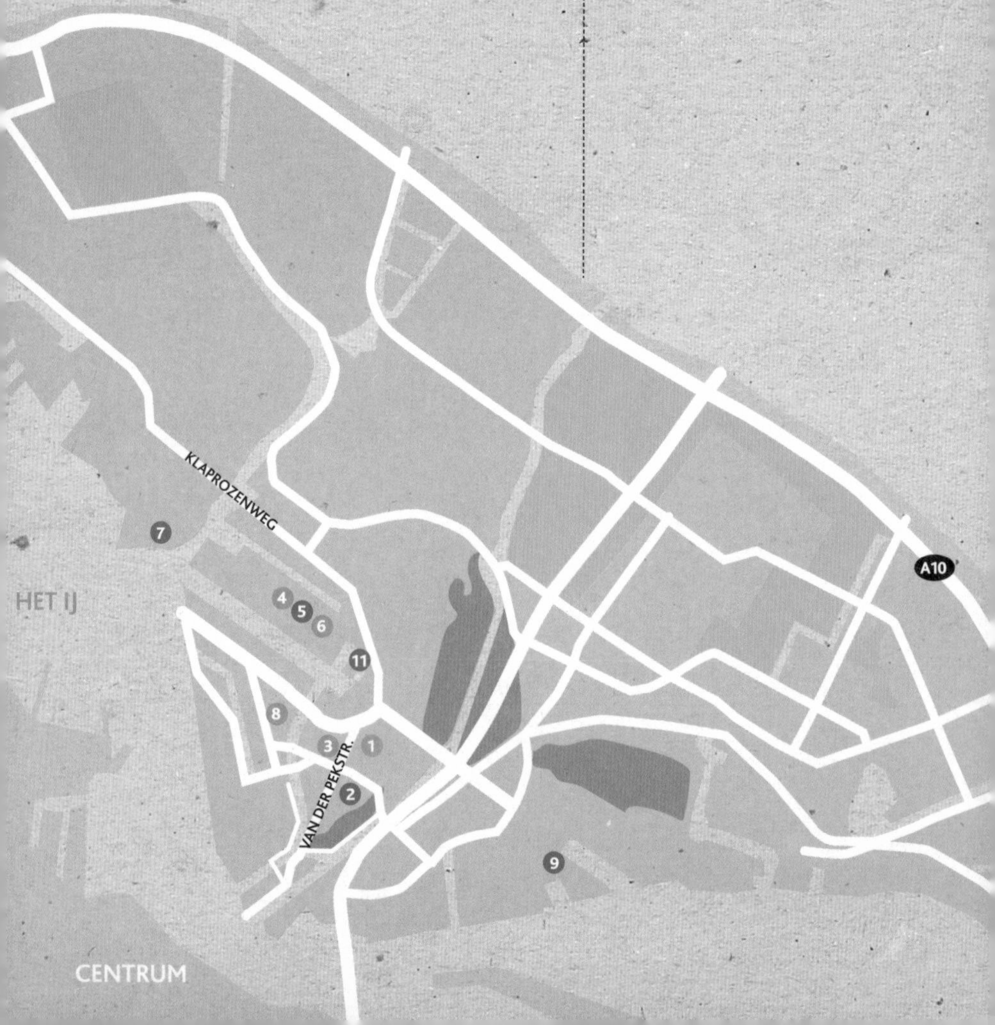

NOORD

Noord (North) is, without a doubt, one of the most lively and inspiring neighbourhoods in the city. Not that long ago, locals wouldn't have dreamed of setting foot on the north embankment, but things have changed. The industrial NDSM wharf has become a breeding ground for cultural entrepreneurs and young creatives. New hangout spots in old factory buildings, and the metamorphosis of the Van der Pek area, have turned this neighbourhood on the other side of the River IJ into the area of choice for many. On weekends and on sunny days, the free ferry service behind Centraal Station heaves with people (and bikes) venturing across the water to catch a movie, or visit one of the many hidden waterfront haunts in this former working-class quarter.

1. PEKMARKT

The market on Van der Pekstraat, held on Wednesdays, Fridays and Saturdays, is one of my favourites. On Fridays, farmers from the surrounding region congregate to sell their organic vegetables, fruit, artisanal breads, beekeepers' honey and homemade sausages and jam. Saturday is the day to search for vintage treasures, handmade objects and other rarities. It's also a great market for weekly groceries — always busy, you'll encounter a mix of locals, vintage lovers and creative types here.

Van der Pekstraat, 1031 Amsterdam
www.pekmarkt.nl

2. CAFÉ MODERN

This restaurant is located in the former Twentsche Bank, a very special building. Entering it feels like stepping back in time to Berlin at the beginning of the twentieth century. The homey décor, all white and vintage, creates a serene atmosphere. The four-course meal made with seasonal produce is delicious. Go downstairs into the old bank vaults to see the temporary art exhibitions. (The owner assures me the thick vault doors won't close while you're in there.)

Meidoornweg 2, 1031 GG Amsterdam
020 4940684
www.modernamsterdam.nl

LOT DOUZE

After securing €26,000 through crowdfunding, **LOT DOUZE** opened her own shop on the up-and-coming Van der Pekstraat. This is not your average bookshop: Lot sells a great range of titles, from bestsellers and classics to surprising finds written by emerging authors. It's a buzzing place where people from all over the city come to browse and discuss her latest acquisitions. Lot participates happily and seems to have read every single one of the books in her shop. Some titles have handwritten recommendations stuck to the shelves, with comments from members of the shop's book club.

3. OVER HET WATER
Van der Pekstraat 59, 1031 CS Amsterdam
020 7370533
www.boekhandeloverhetwater.nl

'I love the water
and the diversity
of the buildings:
modern design next
to old warehouses.'

HOW WOULD YOU DESCRIBE AMSTERDAM?

I feel embraced by Amsterdam. Everyone treats you like family here: they tease you like they've known you forever; they see through the façade. It's a charming city. Even the rougher neighbourhoods have their little gems: a gabled roof, a mini park, some flower pots on the balcony.

WHAT'S IN YOUR SECRET ADDRESS BOOK?

Vlieger on the Amstel, a shop stacked to the ceiling with all kinds of paper. The smell is great and the colours and patterns wonderful. That's where I go to treat myself. Also Jan de Grote Kleinvakman on the Albert Cuypstraat, a long, very narrow haberdashery shop. Even if you're hopeless at embroidery, like me, it's a lovely shop.

WHERE DO YOU GO TO FIND INSPIRATION?

To the IJ. Just crossing the water on the ferry helps me clear my head. The openness of the water and the diversity of the buildings: modern design next to old warehouses and industrial halls. For an energy boost, I take the historical ferry tour on the IJ-buurtveer or go for a walk along the boulevard.

WHAT'S YOUR FAVOURITE AREA?

Ooh, that's a hard one. I like cycling all over
the city because I keep finding new things
and discovering streets I didn't know before.
Amsterdam keeps surprising me. Even the
residential areas, where no tourist ever goes,
have so much charm.

WHAT'S STILL ON YOUR TO-DO LIST?

One day I hope to spend the night with
my partner in the Amrâthhotel in the
Scheepvaarthuis. I can't help but give it longing
looks whenever I pass by it. When you're inside,
you can feel the heart of Amsterdam's history:
the shipping industry.

WHAT IS ABSOLUTELY NOT TO BE
MISSED IN AMSTERDAM?

The garden at the Rijksmuseum. It's a little
hideaway – entry is free – where the noise of
the city dies down and you enter an ordered
ornamental garden with fountains, statues
and old trees. An oasis. It's almost like you're
in Paris.

4. NEEF LOUIS

Old factory lights, industrial Gispen desks, vintage crockery – Neef Louis is a paradise for vintage design lovers. You can rummage around this pair of old halls for hours on end without any distraction. This is where stylists come to rent props for photo shoots. Next door you'll find Van Dijk & Ko (see page 77) for even more vintage goodies. After your vintage shopping spree, head to neighbouring Waargenoegen for a fair-trade coffee or a glass of fresh beetroot juice (see page 76). It's easy to get here: from Centraal Station, it's a 15-minute ride on the ferry to the NDSM wharf.

Papaverweg 46–48, 1032 KJ Amsterdam
020 4869354
www.neeflouis.nl

5. WAARGENOEGEN

Waargenoegen is Hippie heaven, and the perfect place for a rest after your vintage shopping spree at Van Dijk & Ko (see opposite) and Neef Louis (see page 75). Order a fair-trade coffee or a rhubarb juice – owner Thaïs makes just about all of the organic products herself. Her coconut soup is divine, but then so are the toasties and her famous apple pie. The gypsy-style vintage décor suits the industrial character of the area perfectly. The outside terrace is lovely in summer for watching the busy bees at the NDSM wharf do their thing.

Papaverweg 46, 1032 KJ Amsterdam
www.waargenoegen.nl

HONGAARS LIN

MEELZAK

TAFELKLEED

6. VAN DIJK & KO

The go-to place for stylists and vintage-lovers, Van Dijk & Ko sells second-hand designer products, farmhouse and country-style furniture and recycled glass. The enormous hall, located on the old NSDM site is filled floor to ceiling with Hungarian lidded benches, enamel pots and used art and science books. Hours go by in this shop before you know it. For more vintage finds, visit Neef Louis (see page 75) next door then stop for a piece of the famous apple pie at Waargenoegen (opposite).

**Papaverweg 46, 1032 KJ Amsterdam
020 6841524
www.vandijkenko.nl**

7. PLLEK

Many of the city's creatives find their way to this hangout on the waterfront of the IJ. Pllek consists of stacked old sea containers, creating a raw and industrial setting. In summer, you can eat dinner (nearly all the food is local and organic) while seated at one of the long picnic tables outside on the beach, overlooking the city. They stage regular performances and run yoga classes. On hot summer days, they even organise beach massages! From Centraal Station, take the ferry to the NDSM wharf and fifteen minutes later, you're there.

TT Neveritaweg 59, 1033 WB Amsterdam
020 2900020
www.pllek.nl

8. BLOM & BLOM

Brothers Martijn and Kamiel – who lived in Berlin for years – share a passion for lost objects from the former GDR. Together they searched deserted factory buildings for the industrial lamps, desks, glass objects and lab instruments sold in their shop. Wherever they go, they try to find the story behind each item and take pictures to preserve its history. In their shop, these images are displayed next to the objects and whatever you purchase comes with it's own "passport", detailing it's unique history.

Chrysantenstraat 20A, 1031 HT Amsterdam
020 7372691
www.blomandblom.com

9. HOTEL DE GOUDFAZANT

Hotel de Goudfazant is located in an old warehouse on the waterfront. Despite the name, this is a restaurant, not a hotel, and it's been serving good, no-nonsense food for years. The interior is very industrial with sky-high ceilings, and there are always a few vintage cars parked nearby to remind you that this used to be a garage. The restaurant attracts guests from all over the city, not just for the food but also for the views and sunsets from the sunny terrace.

Aambeeldstraat 10H, 1021 KB Amsterdam
020 6365170
www.hoteldegoudfazant.nl

10. LANDMARKT

This covered market is a foodie's paradise. All products come straight from the source, be it farmers, growers, butchers, fishmongers or bakers. Take your time to stroll around and sample the fare, or have a seat at the small restaurant for a salad or a sandwich. In summer, the peaceful terrace on the waterfront opens. Don't forget to cycle back past the idyllic houses on the Schellingwouderdijk and enjoy the breathtaking views across the IJ. A smaller Landmarkt outlet can be found in De Pijp (Van Woustraat 103).

Schellingwouderdijk 339, 1023 NK Amsterdam
020 4904333 (markt)
www.landmarkt.nl

SOMS WAT KLEINER ALTIJD VOL VAN SMAAK

11. CAFÉ DE CEUVEL

This chilled-out waterside café, located in a former shipyard and founded by a group of youngsters, is almost fully sustainable. They turn kitchen waste into gas, the plants that grow everywhere clean the soil and the roof doubles as a greenhouse. The café itself was built using recycled materials, such as eighty-year-old mooring posts from the port of Amsterdam. They serve delicious homemade lemonade and sandwiches – pure food is what it's all about here. In summer you can relax in a hammock or sit on one of the boat benches made by an artist in the workshop opposite. Don't forget to check out the old houseboats that are now on dry land.

Korte Papaverweg 4, 1032 KB Amsterdam
020 2296210
www.cafedeceuvel.nl

SHOPPING

2 CHARLIE + MARY
3 ALL THE LUCK IN THE WORLD
8 COTTONCAKE
9 KAUFHAUS
11 GATHERSHOP
12 HUTSPOT

EATING & DRINKING

1 VENKEL
5 COFFEE & COCONUTS
6 SIR HUMMUS
7 MANA MANA
10 TRUST

RELAXING

4 BART OLIE

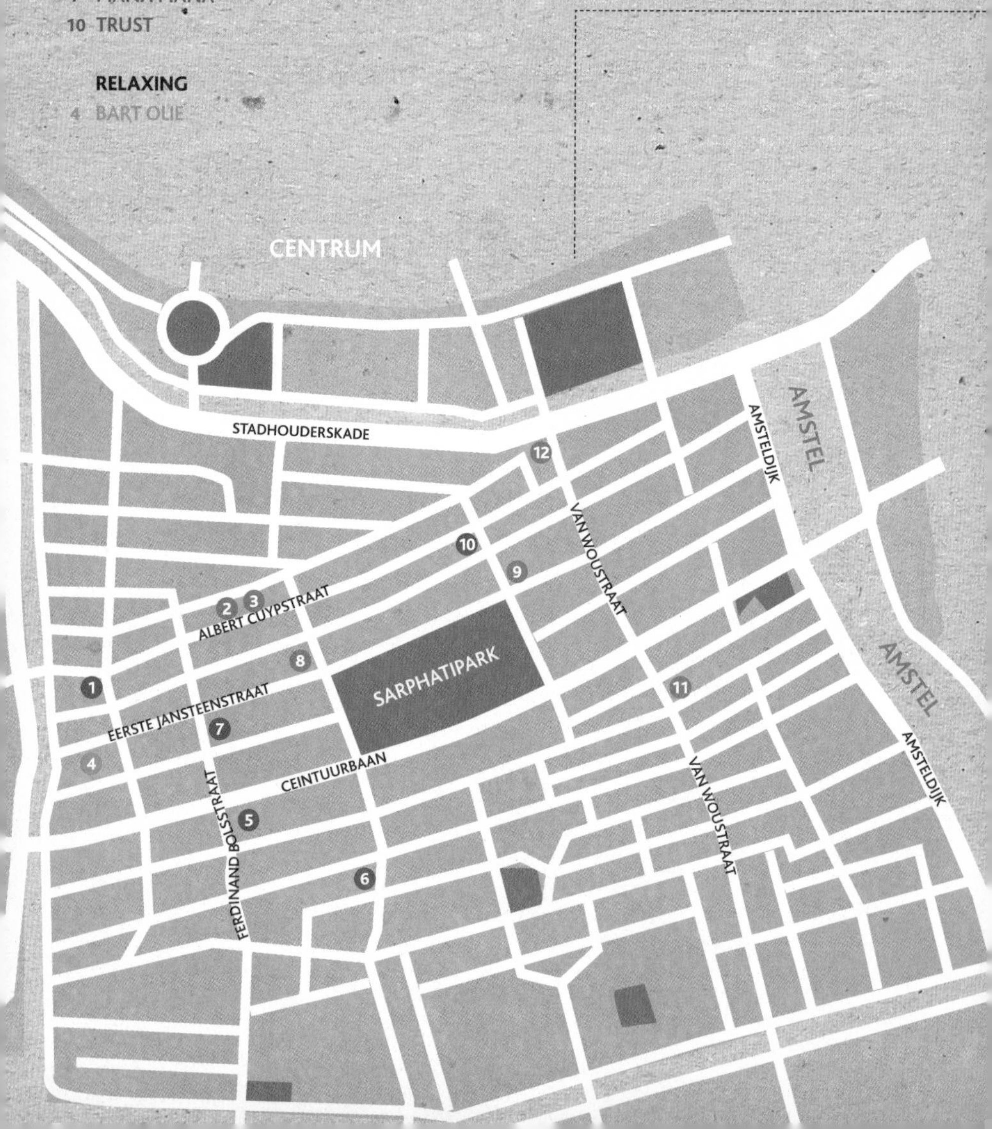
CENTRUM
STADHOUDERSKADE
AMSTEL
AMSTELDIJK
VAN WOUSTRAAT
ALBERT CUYPSTRAAT
SARPHATIPARK
EERSTE JANSTEENSTRAAT
CEINTUURBAAN
FERDINAND BOLSSTRAAT
VAN WOUSTRAAT
AMSTEL
AMSTELDIJK

DE PIJP

De Pijp is a pretty neighbourhood that is easily travelled on foot.
This former working-class quarter has been popular with creatives
and visitors to Amsterdam for decades. Its buildings are close together
and the Albert Cuypmarkt, a daily market where stallholders loudly
advertise their wares, has been located here for the past hundred years.
This is the real Amsterdam, and its many shops and restaurants make
this a much-loved part of the city. You won't find this many inspiring
places packed so tightly anywhere else. Don't skip the side streets off
the Ceintuurbaan, they are full of cute little shops.

1. VENKEL

Fancy a super-healthy salad? You'll find Venkel just a short walk away from the always lovely Albert Cuypmarkt. It serves delicious salads made with fruit and vegetables delivered each morning by local farmers and stacked in this tiny space. One nearby farm grows organic seasonal produce especially for this restaurant. Ask owner Elnaz, she'll happily tell you all about it. The homemade rhubarb and mint cordials for sale in the small shop are not to be missed.

Albert Cuypstraat 22, 1072 CT Amsterdam
020 7723198
www.venkelsalades.nl

CHARLOTTE VAN WAES AND MARIEKE VINCK

True fashion lovers **CHARLOTTE** and **MARIEKE**, owners of Charlie + Mary on the lively Gerard Doustraat, sell only ethical clothing brands like Studio JUX, Veja and People Tree. They love sharing the stories behind their clothes, and reminding people that fashion is so much more than just a piece of clothing. Charlotte and Marieke care about the creative process as well as the philosophy behind their brands, the people who have created them and the materials being used. It's no surprise that stylists and fashion magazines borrow items from the Charlie + Mary collection.

2. CHARLIE + MARY
Gerard Doustraat 84, 1072 VW Amsterdam
020 6628281
www.charliemary.com

> 'We love the city's parks, where people meet when the weather's nice.'

HOW WOULD YOU DESCRIBE THE 'AMSTERDAM STYLE'?

Amsterdam has everything that a great city should have: museums, great coffee and cocktail bars, good restaurants and markets. At the same time, Amsterdam is small-scale and cosy. You can get across town in half an hour. We love the parks and the lifestyle that comes with them, the community gardens where people meet when the weather's nice. We use the small, independent coffee shops as our own personal living rooms.

WHAT'S IN YOUR SECRET ADDRESS BOOK?

When we want to flee the madness of the city, we head to tHUIS aan de AMSTEL. This café/restaurant in a beautiful old house falls just within the city borders but it feels like you're away from it all and the views over the river Amstel are fantastic. When we're feeling cosmopolitan, we go to Panache for delicious food made with ingredients from the nearby Ten Katemarkt and using sustainable fish.

WHERE DO YOU GO TO FIND INSPIRATION?

To the Foam Photography Museum or the Stedelijk Museum. We want to tell the story behind fashion in the same way that photography and art use images to tell a story or convey a message.

WHAT'S YOUR FAVOURITE AREA?
De Pijp. There is so much happening here. There's the traditional Albert Cuypmarkt, loads of Turkish and Surinam delis and more and more young entrepreneurs are starting their businesses here. This has resulted in a vibrant area filled with independent shops, cafés, galleries and lunch spots.

WHAT'S STILL ON YOUR TO-DO LIST?
We want to go to Ruigoord, an artists' village on the edge of town. In summer, it's a really cool festival venue. It's a must-do for everyone living in Amsterdam.

WHAT IS ABSOLUTELY NOT TO BE MISSED IN AMSTERDAM?
Taking the ferry to Noord and having a drink in one of the hotspots along the waterfront: Eye, Pllek, Tolhuistuin or De Ceuvel. That feeling you get when you're on open water and the views over the city from the other side are impressive and romantic.

3. ALL THE LUCK IN THE WORLD

This shop is worth a visit for the interior styling alone. Mother Jane (a graphic designer) and daughter Nina (a goldsmith) both have a keen eye for interior design and pretty things. They sell a lot of vintage items, homewares (Danish design) and handmade lovelies, like postcards, small bits of art and products from young designers. Jane is always on the lookout for new finds for the shop, and Nina designs all the jewellery.

ALL THE LUCK IN THE WORLD
Gerard Doustraat 86, 1072 VW Amsterdam
www.alltheluckintheworld.nl

4. BART OLIE

Tired from walking around all day? Give yourself a break and go for a relaxing massage at Bart Olie. Bart is a pro when it comes to aromatics and their effects on the body. He uses products by brands such as Alqvimia, which are created from natural sources. Bart also makes house calls – you may see him cycling around on his 'bakfiets' (cargo bike) on his way to a lucky customer. He's also well known for his in-company massages.

Eerste Jan Steenstraat 26E, 1072 NL Amsterdam
020 6752175
www.bartolie.nl

5. COFFEE & COCONUTS

This creative spot is located in a former cinema from the twenties. Make sure you have a look, if only for the breathtaking décor, rough walls, high ceilings and natural materials used throughout. It's an inspirational venue for stylists. You can settle in one of the beanbag chairs with a freshly squeezed juice and a piece of cake – nearly all sustenance is organic. Or you can bring your laptop and work; some days it looks like a co-operative workspace. My best tip: order their coconut water and drink it straight from the coconut.

Ceintuurbaan 282-284, 1072 GK Amsterdam
020 3541104
www.ctamsterdam.nl

6. SIR HUMMUS

In their student days, brothers Guy and Lior (originally from Jerusalem) started making the most delicious hummus for their friends. Now it's how they earn their living. This is the only eatery completely dedicated to hummus in the city and you can order hummus (without any additives!) to eat in, or to go. They make everything from scratch using organic chickpeas and a secret recipe, and you can tell. You'll never want to buy a ready-made supermarket version again.

Van der Helstplein 2, 1072 PH Amsterdam
020 6647055
www.sirhummus.nl

7. MANA MANA

This hidden gem attracts vegetarians from all over the city. Owner Omri serves the most delicious falafel, hummus and other Israeli dishes from the open kitchen in this miniscule restaurant. Seats are limited, giving the restaurant a homey, friendly feel. Are you a real carnivore? Omri may even grill a skewer of meat for you. On Saturdays, you'll find him selling his hummus from a stall at the cosy market on the Lindegracht.

**Eerste Jan Steenstraat 85, 1072 NE Amsterdam
06 41631098**

8. COTTONCAKE

From this typically long, narrow room (called a 'pijpela' or pipe drawer), Tessa and Jorinde only sell things that they really like. They love travelling and bringing back new and unique items for their shop from every trip. They stock wonderful brands such as Storm & Marie, Minus, and Samsoe & Samsoe, and they get very excited about up-and-coming (often local) labels they discover. Their smoothies and homemade banana and walnut cake are pretty decent, too. Have a bite and enjoy the temporary art exhibitions on the walls (the art is also for sale).

1e van der Helststraat 76, 1072 NZ Amsterdam
020 7895838
www.cottoncake.nl

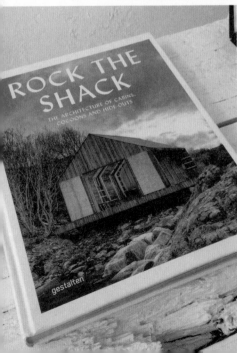

PRINT CEBINE € 24,90

9. KAUFHAUS

This is where you find some of the better vintage pieces in Amsterdam. No threadbare dresses with giant shoulder pads here, but rather beautifully cut pieces, pure wool and pretty patterns. Morena and her two friends have a great sense of fashion and styling, and they source every item of clothing and each bag themselves. The same goes for the vintage furniture they sell. It's nice to know that half their profits go to a charity project in Africa.

**Eerste Sweelinckstraat 21H, 1073 CL Amsterdam
www.hetkaufhaus.nl**

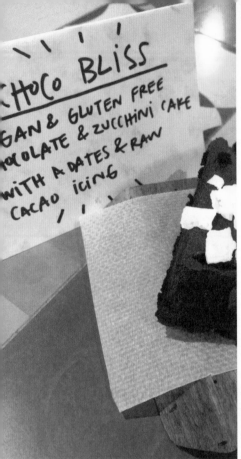

10. TRUST

This friendly eatery has a remarkable motto: come as you are, pay as you feel. Seven friends came up with the concept. You'll find a copy of *Een cursus in wonderen* (A course in miracles) on every table – the world of love and happiness described in the book is mirrored in the quotes on the walls of the café. You'll find mouthwatering organic soups, salads, homemade cakes and smoothies on the menu, sporting names like 'down the rabbit hole'. There are no price tags – you pay what you deem fair for whatever you consume.

Albert Cuypstraat 210, 1073 BM Amsterdam
020 7371532
www.trustamsterdam.org

11. GATHERSHOP

Owner Jessica is a designer by trade and this is immediately visible in her serene little shop. Jessica believes in simplicity and sells only handmade items: ceramics, jewellery, frames, postcards and other trinkets with a story. They're all made by largely unknown designers (many from Amsterdam) who work in small studios. The shop is beautifully styled and definitely worth a visit. If you want to be inspired, follow her on Instagram @gathershop.

Van Woustraat 99, 1074 AG Amsterdam
020 7520681
www.gathershop.nl

12. HUTSPOT

The creativity and freedom of the city is evident in this concept store. Downstairs you'll find unique clothes, jewellery, home accessories and art – from young designers as well as established brands. Upstairs there's a coffee bar and a place to have lunch surrounded by pretty things. From early morning, the place is flooded with people who come here to work in peace. This is where you can really savour the urban lifestyle of Amsterdam. Before you head out, check out the latest (often surprising) art exhibitions by young artists and photographers.

Van Woustraat 4, 1073 LL Amsterdam
020 2231331
Rozengracht 204–210, 1016 NL Amsterdam
020 3708708
www.hutspotamsterdam.com

Sidamo

SHAKISSO FARM
LICHT
FRUITIG
CHOCOLADE
ELEGANT
ETHIOPIE

SHOPPING
1 POMPON
2 HET BRILLENPALEIS
4 PICCOLA
5 LENA
8 MOOOI
12 SPRMRKT

EATING & DRINKING
6 WINKEL
7 KOEVOET
9 SLA
13 DE VEGETARISCHE
TRAITEUR

CULTURE & RELAXING
10 DE NIEUWE YOGASCHOOL
11 GALERIE BART

MARKETS
3 NOORDERMARKT

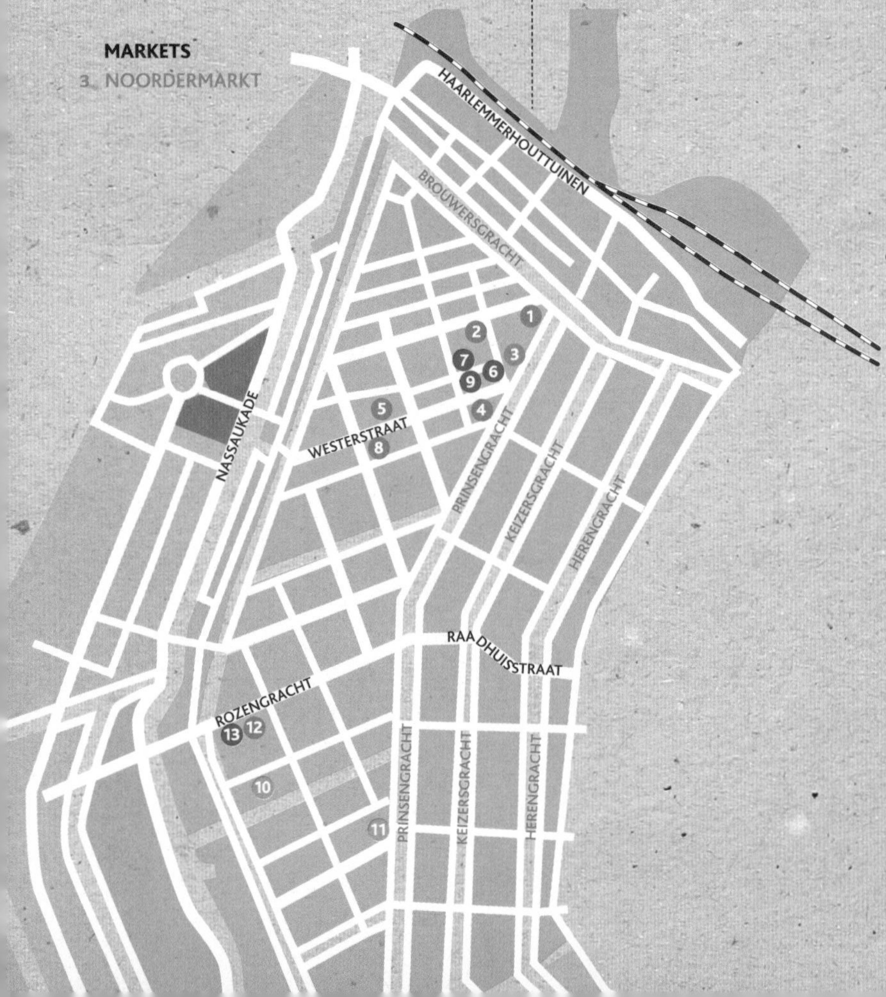

DE JORDAAN

De Jordaan is the ideal neighbourhood to get lost in. There are small alleys to explore, canals to follow, tiny houses and hidden courtyards to discover, and gabled roofs to admire. There are also countless small restaurants and little boutiques selling rarities, vintage treasures, clothes and flowers, and there are some genuine local bakeries and butchers still operating in this part of town. The Saturday farmers' market at Noordermarkt is lively and fun, with regional farmers selling organic produce.

1. POMPON

Pompon is more than just a local florist, it's also one of the most stylish flower shops in the city. The shop floor is crammed with beautiful blooms and plants, and the staff can create the most stunning flower arrangements to order. This family company supplies stylists with flowers for photo shoots and is the go-to place for big events (like the coronation of the Dutch king) and for the well-off ladies living in the pretty canalside townhouses.

Prinsengracht 8–10, 1015 DV Amsterdam
020 6225137
www.pompon.nl

2. HET BRILLENPALEIS

Looking through the shop window, you could
be fooled into thinking this store selling
vintage spectacle frames from the sixties and
seventies has long since closed down. There
are sunglasses and frames scattered around
on tabletops, along the windowsill and in the
shop window. The owner is an avid collector of
unused(!) retro frames from Italy, France and
the UK. If you, like me, love unusual sunglasses,
this shop is paradise. Unfortunately, it is only
open on Saturdays.

Noorderkerkstraat 18, 1015 NB Amsterdam

3. NOORDERMARKT

Every Saturday, my favourite farmers' market is held under the lime trees of Noordermarkt Square. It's a real meeting point for locals, the way a market should be. Many of the stands sell organic produce, from vegetables and fruit to bread and dairy. Others sell vintage things, pretty jewellery and rare books. If you need a rest from strolling around, take a seat on the sunny terrace of Winkel (see page 127).

Noordermarkt, Amsterdam
www.boerenmarktamsterdam.nl

SPeLt
500gr. €2.00
615

GORt
500gr. 2.00

4. PICCOLA

Jewellery designer Noomi van Gelder creates silver and gemstone jewellery inspired by the symbolism of many different cultures. Noomi's workshop is located on an unassuming street corner near the Noordermarkt, so be careful you don't walk by and miss it. The necklaces, armbands, earrings and rings are all handmade, and if you're looking for something with a personal touch, Noomi will seek out the right gemstones for you.

Prinsengracht 16, 1015 DV Amsterdam
06 288646769
www.noomivangelder.nl

SUZANNE SMULDERS

Owners **SUZANNE**, **ELISA**, **ANGELA** and **DIANA** run the first fashion library in Amsterdam, where you can borrow beautiful vintage clothes, items from emerging designers and high-quality eco-labels. These fashion lovers want to add their penny's worth when it comes to sustainable living. For a monthly fee (or using prepaid vouchers) you can borrow as many dresses, coats, cardigans and hats as you like. If there's something that really takes your fancy, you can also buy it.

5. LENA
Westerstraat 174H, 1015 MP Amsterdam
020 7891781
www.lena-library.com

'Amsterdam is crazy and extreme, and I love it.'

WHAT DOES AMSTERDAM MEAN TO YOU?

All four of us are originally from Eindhoven and I can tell you, Amsterdam is quite different. You can be that little bit more crazy and extreme, which is good fun. Amsterdam is the better place to be, especially when it comes to our passion: vintage. I am relieved to find so many second-hand goods for sale here. Seeking out unique and good-quality pieces is a wonderful thing to do in Amsterdam.

WHAT'S IN YOUR SECRET ADDRESS BOOK?

Oh my, there are so many nice places. I love drinking a double order of coffee and acai berry juice in the sun at Brazuca on the Rijnstraat – typically Brazilian. But I also love walking my dog in the Amsterdamse Bos (Amsterdam Forest) when it's sunny.

WHERE DO YOU GO TO FIND INSPIRATION?

I mostly find inspiration in people, and we have enough of them here in Amsterdam. The garden at the Rijksmuseum is a favourite of mine for reading and watching the world go by – the people by the fountain are especially amusing to watch.

WHAT'S YOUR FAVOURITE AREA?
Tough question, but I think I'll go for De Pijp, where I live. It's a little less hectic than the city centre, but it's full of great places to eat, drink and shop. De Pijp has a mixture of trendy restaurants, second-hand shops, concept stores, multicultural hotspots and old-fashioned pubs. And, of course, the Albert Cuypmarkt is around the corner.

WHAT IS ABSOLUTELY NOT TO BE MISSED IN AMSTERDAM?
If you like films, go to De Uitkijk cinema, the oldest film theatre in the Netherlands with twenties-style décor. There's only one screen, with balcony seats, and the staff waits on you while you watch the film.

6. WINKEL

This coffee and lunch spot, located in a store with a typical Amsterdam split-level interior, is known for its unbeatable apple pie. Fresh pies are baked around the clock, even on busy Saturdays when they open extra early, at 7 am, for the farmers' market. As soon as the sun comes out in spring, the terrace is permanently occupied by locals in the know: at Winkel you can sit in the sun all day long.

Noordermarkt 43, 1015 NA Amsterdam
020 6230223
www.winkel43.nl

7. KOEVOET

Curious to know how the people in De Jordaan live their lives behind those tasselled and fringed curtains? Head to Koevoet, an Italian restaurant in a narrow street behind the Noordermarkt, where owners Mario and Piergiorgio have left everything untouched. It's like stepping back a century in time, into the pub of the Koevoet family in the year 1900. For years, they have been serving delicious and authentic Italian dishes (no pizza though). I can recommend everything on the menu – the fresh mozzarella is especially divine. This is a hidden gem frequented by locals. Don't leave without having a scroppino, beaten by hand at your table.

Lindenstraat 17, 1015 KV Amsterdam
020 6240846
www.koevoetamsterdam.com

129

m o o o i

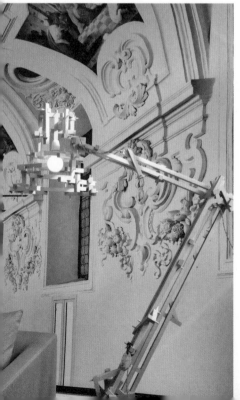

8. MOOOI

Designer Marcel Wanders runs a gallery and design shop in an old school building in the middle of De Jordaan. It's a place you can happily browse for hours, filled with beautiful furniture, lamps, rugs, vases, art and other pretty things designed by Marcel himself, or by other leading designers such as Piet Boon, Jaime Hayon and Edward van Vliet. I'd visit for the high ceilings and the huge windows alone.

Westerstraat 187, 1015 MA Amsterdam
020 5287760
www.moooi.com

9. SLA

If you're a fan of salads, you'll love this place. The greens aren't just on the menu – they're on the walls and tables, too. You can put together your own dish from the greenhouse-shaped salad bar, or opt for one of the chef's concoctions. The place gets quite busy around lunchtime, but you can always order your salad to take away and eat it sitting on a bench on the Noordermarkt, where there's always something interesting going on.

Westerstraat 34, 1015 MK Amsterdam
020 3702733
For more locations, check www.ilovesla.com

10. DE NIEUWE YOGASCHOOL

The former Armenschool (meaning 'poor people's school') in the middle of the neighbourhood now houses a yoga school run by Amsterdam's famous yoga teacher Johan Noorloos. Here, you can take a yoga class or workshop, or have a massage. You can also wander in for a healthy salad, a smoothie or a date in the cosy 'living room'. Somewhat unexpectedly in these city streets, there's an enormous garden at the back where, surrounded by flowers and plants, you can enjoy the silence and the birdsong.

Laurierstraat 109, 1016 PL Amsterdam
www.denieuweyogaschool.nl

11. GALERIE BART

This gallery focuses on new graduates of the Dutch art schools, with owner Bart visiting all final year exhibitions looking for new talent. Extraordinary paintings, objects and video installations feature in its exhibitions. Every year, Bart organises a 'new harvest exhibition', showcasing a selection of the most outstanding art by final year students – students who, according to the gallery, will be shaping the future of art.

Elandsgracht 16, 1016 TW Amsterdam
020 3206208
www.galeriebart.nl

12. SPRMRKT

This building once housed a large supermarket, now it's the place to find beautiful designer brands. The old fridge doors (now the doors of the changing rooms) are the only reminders of this large industrial space's humble beginnings. They sell clothes (men and women's), shoes, jewellery, sunglasses and many brands that are hard to find anywhere else, such as Wendy & Jim and Hennik Vibskov. A large collection of art and photography books, and a hairdressing salon make this location even more special.

Rozengracht 191–193, 1016 LZ Amsterdam
020 3305601
www.sprmrkt.nl

FRONAUTS

E LEGEND OF THE AFRICAN SPACE PROGRAMME

A fully-equipped African waiting the threatening odometer-upturned spaces suit

Photograph by Cristina de Middel, 2012

13. DE VEGETARISCHE TRAITEUR

At first glance it might seem that this caterer has nothing but meat for sale, but in fact all of the sausages, chicken pieces and sausage rolls are made from soy and vegetables. The tuna and fish fingers don't contain any fish either. It's plant-based all the way – the perfect shop for vegetarians, vegans and flexitarians. There are tables for lunch in the back or you can take away a sandwich or a salad and eat it on the bench out front. Culture lovers take note: the building opposite (number 184) is the place that Rembrandt van Rijn called home for a large part of his life.

Rozengracht 217, 1016 NA Amsterdam
020 4234199
www.vegetarischetraiteur.nl

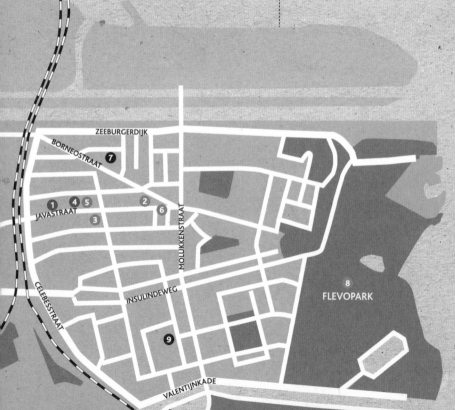

SHOPPING
2 JAVA BOOKSHOP
3 ASHES TO SNOW
5 AMBROZIJN
6 BLOEMEN OP LOCATIE

EATING & DRINKING
1 HARTJE OOST
4 BEDFORD-STUYVESANT

CULTURE & RELAXING
7 STUDIO/K
9 WELLNESS 1926

WALKING
8 FLEVOPARK

ZEEBURGERDIJK
BORNEOSTRAAT
JAVASTRAAT
MOLUKKENSTRAAT
INSULINDEWEG
CELEBESSTRAAT
VALENTIJNKADE
FLEVOPARK

INDISCHE BUURT

Take the underpass that runs beneath the train tracks in
Amsterdam-Oost, the east of the city, to get to the Indische Buurt
(Indies Neighbourhood). Until quite recently, this was one of the
less appealing areas of Amsterdam. But now that the early
twentieth-century houses characteristic of this neighbourhood are
being done up, creative people are flocking to its streets. On the
almost-fully renovated Javastraat, coffee bars and galleries are popping
up like daisies next to local greengrocers' and mobile phone shops.
This surprising mix of shops is exactly what makes this neighbourhood
so attractive. Are you done walking around the Indische Buurt?
Head to the Flevopark, one of the most beautiful yet relatively
undiscovered parks in the city.

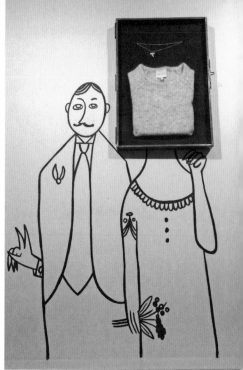

1. HARTJE OOST

Eline and Esther's coffee boutique is a wonderful place to find pretty vintage things and handmade designs, but it's also the place for a coffee and a hummus sandwich. All refreshments are sustainable, organic and local, and made by the owners themselves. The place is always buzzing with locals, who come here to work on their laptops or have a cup of tea and a chat with a friend while sitting at the long table.

Javastraat 23, 1094 GZ Amsterdam
020 2332137
www.hartjeoost.nl

2. JAVA BOOKSHOP

You could almost walk past this cosy bookshop on the busy Javastraat because of its small size. Sharon and Sanne were two of the first people to realise this street would become a hip and happening place. Their shop is like a warm living room, where they serve lovely lattes while you browse their books. Both owners are true bookworms and give great advice. Here, you'll find many unusual books from famous and not-so-famous authors, plus (English language) books on Amsterdam. Don't skip the children's section.

Javastraat 145, 1094 HE Amsterdam
020 4634993
www.javabookshop.nl

MAIKEL PIQUÉ AND MAICHEL KLLICK

These hairdressers worked for years, pop-up style, at festivals, parties and in old school buildings. Now they're running their first proper shop in the multicultural Javastraat. Not only can you get a haircut while sitting at the big round table at the back, you can also drink coffee and feast your eyes on art by young designers. With this shop, these high-end hairdressers have created an artistic hub where there's always something going on. Someone might just start playing the grand piano while you're getting a new 'do.

3. ASHES TO SNOW
Javastraat 72, 1094 HL Amsterdam
020 3621480
www.ashestosnow.com

'It's wonderful to see that the place we've created attracts extraordinary people.'

HOW WOULD YOU DESCRIBE THE 'AMSTERDAM STYLE'?

Amsterdam has so many styles and groups. They're all colourful and diverse. Amsterdam is small but nice.

WHAT'S IN YOUR SECRET ADDRESS BOOK?

The allotments in Noord and the area behind it. It's a haven, so quiet and green with little ditches. The Flevopark is also fantastic – dogs are still allowed to be off-leash there.

WHERE DO YOU GO TO FIND INSPIRATION?

It depends what's happening at that particular time. It could be a concert, exhibition or an event, for example at the Concertgebouw, FOAM or Ruigoord. For fashion and new collections, SPRMRKT is very inspiring. But we mostly find inspiration in the people that sit down in our chairs for a haircut. It's wonderful to see that the place we've created attracts extraordinary people.

WHAT'S YOUR FAVOURITE AREA?
The Indische Buurt. You'll find us on the
Javastraat every single day and it's amazing.
It's a mixed bag and so much happens there.
We're excited to see how things will develop
in the future.

WHAT'S STILL ON YOUR TO-DO LIST?
Roti Room, an Indian restaurant on the Eerste
Oosterparkstraat. It's supposed to be really
good for vegetarians.

**WHAT IS ABSOLUTELY NOT TO BE
MISSED IN AMSTERDAM?**
A picnic in a park with friends on a nice
summer's day.

4. BEDFORD-STUYVESANT

This coffee-slash-lunch-slash-drinks spot on the Javastraat is named after an area in New York's Brooklyn — the once deprived but now achingly hip neighbourhood. The vintage interior alone is worth the bicycle detour into the Indische Buurt. I recommend the spinach smoothies and spelt rolls (and of course the coffee) served with dedication by Eusène and Caroline. The big table is a quiet working place and mums with kids can meet in the cosy children's corner.

Javastraat 55, 1094 HA Amsterdam
020 3342175
www. bedfortstuyvesant.nl

151

5. AMBROZIJN

This artisanal deli is located in the lively Javastraat with its melting pot of cultures. They sell sausages from sausage makers Brandt & Levie, peanut butter from Zeemansboter, surprising organic wines, cakes from Mama bakery, chocolate and pour-your-own olive oil. You can taste the wines at the very back of the deli. This is a friendly neighbourhood shop from the old days, with a modern twist.

Javastraat 75A, 1094 HB Amsterdam
06 34692917
www.ambrozijn.nl

6. BLOEMEN OP LOCATIE

Bloemen op Locatie (meaning 'flowers on location') is more than your ordinary flower shop. It sells flowers by the stem so you can create your own arty bunch, and it organises creative flower-arranging workshops. Stylist Anchela designs the most beautiful arrangements for events and special occasions.

Javaplein 4, 1094 HW Amsterdam
020 4635317
www.bloemenoplocatie.nl

7. STUDIO / K

People from all over the city come here to view the best art-house films (and to enjoy the comfy chairs). Studio/K is not just a cinema, but also a café, restaurant and club. It's located in a former craft guild school with tall windows, and it is run by students. The atmosphere is homey, making it a place to have a beer or simple organic meal all by yourself. The owners have a keen eye for art by emerging artists, which is showcased in temporary exhibitions.

Timorplein 62, 1094 CC Amsterdam
020 6920422
www.studio-k.nu

8. FLEVOPARK

When it was designed at the start of the last century, the architects took inspiration from the parks of Paris and Hamburg. It's one of my favourite parks because it makes you feel like you're in the middle of the French countryside. In summer, it is a melting pot of cultures with families picnicking, children playing and locals soaking up the sun. Take a stroll on the waterfront, past the fishermen's houses and have a rest on the terrace of Het Gemaal — an impossibly pretty spot in the middle of the park — where you can eat, drink and enjoy the peace and quiet.

Park entrance: Javaplantsoen and Valentijnkade

Binnenplaats

Koude dompelbad

Bar

Hot tub

Toiletten

Warme douches

Sauna's

9. WELLNESS 1926

This small city spa is located in the middle of the Indische Buurt, making it an unexpected gem. Owner Samira is an interior decorator and designed the surprising interior herself. It's a mixture of vintage, Mediterranean tiles and magical lights, with halved desk drawers and chairs attached to the walls. Here, you can get a massage, manicure or pedicure and there's even a small sauna. The homey café serves delicious tea, made by Samira herself from the herbs her aunt brings from Morocco.

Halmaheirastraat 28, 1094 RL Amsterdam
020 7749180
www.wellness1926.nl

OOSTERPARK

WIBAUTSTRAAT

AMSTEL

RINGDIJK

MIDDENWEG

FRANKENDAEL
PARK

AMSTEL

OOST & WATERGRAAFSMEER

This area, on the east side of the city, is perfect for getting away from the crowds. Park Frankendael and the Oosterpark (with its monument to filmmaker Theo van Gogh) are quiet compared to the Vondelpark. Until recently, not much was happening in Oost, but lately it has developed it's own 'vibe'. The Transvaalbuurt area is on the up and you'll find the best little shops and restaurants in the narrow side streets off the Beukenplein and the Wibautstraat. Have a walk, or better still, cycle around (the distances are greater here than in other neighbourhoods) and make sure you finish the day on the roof of the cool Volkshotel, which has the best views in the city.

1. MARIT'S HUISKAMER-RESTAURANT

This intimate restaurant is hidden in the living room of a beautiful townhouse in an unassuming street. The house is still lived in, adding to the feeling that you are a guest at the dinner table of hostess Marit. A textile designer by profession, Marit loves to cook so much that she decided to open a small restaurant. Three nights a week she serves her guests the most delicious, sustainable vegetarian dishes. The atmosphere is homey and unpretentious; you'll want to linger here all night. Marit's place only has eight tables, so reservations are a must.

Andreas Bonnstraat 34H, 1091 BA Amsterdam
020 7763864
www.maritshuiskamerrestaurant.nl

2. DOORDEWEEKS

Make-up bars (comfy places where you get pampered before a party, important dinner or after-work drinks by a professional make-up artist) are a trend in both Berlin and New York. The clever minds behind this spot, Jildou and Wiske, have used this trend to give their concept store a unique angle. Once you've browsed the vintage clothes, trendy second-hand furniture and art by emerging talent, you may as well settle in for a cup of coffee, or join the crowd at the lovely lunch table where you can make your own sandwich.

Andreas Bonnstraat 12, 1091 AX Amsterdam
020 8943118
www.doordeweeks.com

3. IJSBOEFJE

In the wee hours of the morning, you'll find DJ Sheila Hill playing her music at the hippest clubs in Amsterdam. During the day, she sells delicious ice cream in her salon on the lively Beukenplein. She designed the homey interior, which uses lots of vintage finds and a Mediterranean tiled wall, with friends. Her family runs the artisan Italian ice-cream factory Monte Pelmo in De Jordaan, where the ice cream for Ijsboefje is also made. During the winter months a friend takes over the place to cook mouth-watering Indian curries.

Beukenplein 5, 1092 BA Amsterdam
020 6638922
www.facebook.com/hetijsboefje

4. DE VERGULDEN EENHOORN

This is where Amsterdam locals come to escape the city crowds. Located in a former city farm from the early eighteenth century, this restaurant feels like a countryside venue in the middle of the city. The gastronomic menu can be enjoyed in the former cow shed. Outside you'll find a large terrace with long picnic tables where you can listen to birdsong until the sun sets. There's also a small bed and breakfast.

Ringdijk 58, 1097 AH Amsterdam
020 2149333
www.verguldeneenhoorn.nl

5. VOLKSHOTEL

This was once the beating editorial heart of one of the largest broadsheet newspapers in the Netherlands. Now it's a hotel, restaurant, café, club and a meeting place for creative people who come here to work and brainstorm. Night owls are welcome too; they're open 24/7. I don't know any other place where the mix is so perfect – locals and tourists exist happily alongside each other. Take the lift to the seventh floor, where club Canvas is located; it has one of the best terraces, with views across town. Hotel guests can use the hot tub at the top of the building.

Wibautstraat 150, 1091 GR Amsterdam
020 2612110
www.volkshotel.nl

6. BETER & LEUK

Owners Hanneke, Maaike and Ilse are true
health nuts, and it shows. Everything that's sold
at Beter & Leuk is homemade: granola, quinoa
salad, banana bread, ginger and beetroot juice.
This concept cafe is fully sustainable. The
chairs and tables are vintage or made from
sustainable materials. In the back you'll find
changing collections of eco-friendly clothing,
jewellery, art and books. In the evenings, when
the shop is closed, they run a vegan sushi-
making workshop.

1e Oosterparkstraat 91, 1091 GW Amsterdam
020 7670029
www.beterenleuk.nl

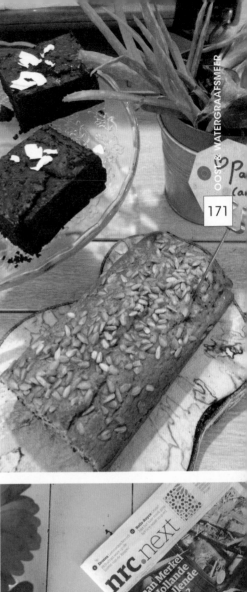

JEROEN KEIZER

For the best cranberry cake or pumpkin pie, head to this neighbourhood gem in the emerging Transvaalbuurt. All pastries are homemade and baked in the open kitchen behind the small coffee shop. Owner **JEROEN** imports the coffee beans from Brazil and roasts them himself. Rum Baba opens early for breakfast and lunch. It's alive with young locals drinking their first latte of the day.

7. RUM BABA
Pretoriusstraat 33, 1092 EX Amsterdam
020 8469498
facebook.com/RumBabaBakes

'Oost is developing and thriving, but it still has that raw edge.'

HOW WOULD YOU DESCRIBE THE 'AMSTERDAM STYLE'?

On the one hand, Amsterdam feels like a large village, but on the other hand it's a city with close links to the rest of the world, with many cultures and a worldly influence.

WHAT'S IN YOUR SECRET ADDRESS BOOK?

Hakata Senpachi, a Japanese eatery near to the RAI exhibition centre, due to their legendary octopus balls and lukewarm sake, served in wooden bowls that are too full not to spill.

WHERE DO YOU GO TO FIND INSPIRATION?

To the American Book Center. I don't have the time to travel the world, but here I find a world of inspiration, ranging from design and food to literature.

WHAT'S YOUR FAVOURITE AREA?

Oost. From the moment we landed here, the area has been developing and thriving, but it still has that raw edge to it. It has a mixture of people, entrepreneurs and cultures.

WHAT'S STILL ON YOUR TO-DO LIST?

I'd like to attend a chocolate-tasting session at Chocolátl. It's a chance to experience chocolate the way I experience coffee and tea: all the way from the berries, through to the processing and preparation and into your mouth.

8. KLEIN BERLIJN

This vintage shop is an ode to the real
Berlin, in all its raw glory. Once a traditional
apothecary, you can now rummage through
handmade clothes, jewellery, vintage shoes
and bags, and other bits and bobs. Its chaotic
feel and extraordinary treasures evoke a Berlin
sensibility. Tea lovers will thoroughly enjoy the
enormous assortment of loose-leaf teas.

Middenweg 36, 1097 BP Amsterdam
06 28688046
www.kleinberlijn.com

9. HANDMADE HEAVEN

Are you a fan of paper, thread and felt? Then don't miss this arts and crafts paradise. Interior stylist Twirre sells all possible kinds of beads, clay, paper, DIY kits and many pretty books (children's books, too). She regularly organises workshops on techniques such as stamping, flower felting and weaving. This craft store contains so many lovely things, you won't know what to choose. This is the place where hip mothers from Watergraafsmeer go to buy their children's birthday gifts.

Middenweg 31, 1098 AB Amsterdam
020 6630309
www.handmade-heaven.nl

10. PIEKSMAN

Owners and brothers Yvo and Ulco only stock top wines. They import organic wines from more than eighty vineyards, mainly in France and Italy. They test everything they sell themselves. The shop is a true neighbourhood meeting place, where you'll find yourself chatting away about daily life in the green Watergraafsmeer area.

Hogeweg 19, 1098 BV Amsterdam
020 8203602
www.pieksman.nl

11. HET BAKBLIK

Every Wednesday, Christina drives her old Renault 4 around Watergraafsmeer to sell her homemade lemon butterfly biscuits, white chocolate cake, little lavender cakes, oat cookies and other sweet things. The smell of freshly baked goods wafts from the back of her car; it's as if you're picking up a little cake at your grandmother's. Christina bakes everthing herself, using natural ingredients. Check her Facebook page to find out where her mobile cake shop will be popping up that day.

facebook.com/vanmoss.nl
06 14495051

HET BAKBLIK

DE RIJDENDE TAARTENWINKEL

12. LEMONADE

Owner Sabrine is always on the lookout for cute and cool kids' clothing. Her shop stocks a lot of Danish and Dutch children's designer collections. They also sell nice gifts and home accessories from, among others, HK Living and House Doctor. At the back of the shop, there's a small espresso bar and in summer the mini terrace outside gets put to good use.

Middenweg 46HS, 1097 BR Amsterdam
020 7526555
www.mylemonade.nl

13. BOEKALICIOUS

This is a really special bakery/cookbook store.
Here, you can eat homemade cakes, Loustain
macarons(!) and artisan bread rolls, while
drinking locally roasted coffee and rummaging
through a bookcase full of cookbooks and
culinary fiction. Owner and publisher Jacqueline
Smit loves reading, cooking and bringing
people with similar interests together in her
comfortable living room. The bakery closes
at 3 pm but there's still plenty to do after
that: famous writers drop by for readings
and Jacqueline organises children's cookery
workshops and tastings.

Galileïplantsoen 94, 1098 NC Amsterdam
020 3586383
www.boekalicious.nl

14. THUIS AAN DE AMSTEL

This culinary and arty cafe is a green oasis unlike any other in the city. It's located in the former engineer's residence of the Zuidergasfabriek (meaning 'southern gas factory'), on an industrial estate filled with beautiful buildings. The interior is decked out with vintage and up-cycled furniture, its many knick knacks hint at the building's history. tHUIS aan de AMSTEL boasts one of the sunniest terraces in the city, with a view of the wide Amstel river. It's a bit of a bike ride to get there (mooring a boat out front is a possibility, too), but it's worth it. There's also an ongoing exhibition featuring local artists.

Korte Ouderkerkerdijk 45, 1096 AC Amsterdam
020 3547520
www.thuisaandeamstel.nl

SHOPPING
1 GEKAAPT (MOBILE SHOP)
5 WILDERNIS
6 CREATIEVE GARAGE
12 FRIDAY NEXT

EATING & DRINKING
3 FOODHALLEN
4 PAUL ANNÉE
8 HOLY RAVIOLI
9 JAN SCHILDER
11 DE FIETSKANTINE
13 KOFFIE ACADEMIE

CULTURE
7 FILMHALLEN
10 LAB111

MARKETS
2 LOCAL GOODS MARKET

DE CLERCQSTRAAT
BILDERDIJKSTRAAT
NASSAUKADE
KINKERSTRAAT
1E CONSTANTIJN HUYGENS STRAAT
OVERTOOM
VONDELPARK

OUD-WEST

Oud-West (Old West) is one of the most diverse neighbourhoods in Amsterdam. Business people, creative types, students, families with small children and pensioners all live here, making it a lovely and lively area. Oud-West is just around the corner from the city centre, but isn't nearly as touristy as, for example, De Pijp. The streets around the Bellamyplein still have a village-like character and the houses have cute gardens out front. Take a walk along the Overtoom and the Jan Pieter Heijestraat to the Kinkerstraat and explore a wealth of small, undiscovered shops, coffee bars and other hangouts. Finish your walk at De Hallen, a former tram depot where you can eat street food in the style of London's Borough Market, catch a movie or spoil yourself at the lovely little shops.

1. GEKAAPT

They call themselves a travelling circus of brands and designers, popping up in different locations all over the city. They'll hijack an empty building, create a warm and welcoming atmosphere and make a mean coffee. At Gekaapt (meaning 'hijacked') you'll find beautiful eco-friendly clothes, handmade jewellery, sustainable home accessories, vintage design and a lot of plants. The designers man the coffee bar themselves and are keen to share the stories behind their products. Check the website to find their current location.

www.gekaapt.nu

2. LOCAL GOODS MARKET

In the large passage of De Hallen, around the corner from the daily Ten Katemarkt, is a weekly Saturday market with products designed or made in and around Amsterdam – from bicycles to clothes, and bags to furniture. There are also stalls selling tea, sausages and chocolate. The atmosphere is good and, because it's a covered market, it's nearly always on, rain or shine. This same passage also houses the Local Goods Store, a shop selling several local brands that are also part of the weekly market.

Hannie Dankbaar Passage 33, 1053 RT Amsterdam
www.dezwijger.nl

3. FOODHALLEN

This indoor food market is located in an old tram depot that lay abandoned for years before it was brought back to life. Borough Market in London and the Mercado de San Miguel in Madrid, two immensely popular food markets, were the inspiration for this concept. Foodies who love their street food will find themselves at home here. Stalls selling food from all corners of the world offer everything from Australian meat pies to Vietnamese delicacies, sushi rolls and hog roasts. I like drinking coffee here for that big-city feel.

Bellamyplein 51, 1053 AT Amsterdam
www.foodhallen.nl

FOODHALLEN

4. PAUL ANNÉE

For the past fifty years, this small bakery has baked bread the way grandmothers used to. Everything they sell is organic, vegetarian and free from refined sugar. In the sixties, this was a hippie haunt. You won't find your usual bakery suspects here – that's not their style. I recommend the homemade tofu rolls. You won't find them anywhere else in the city.

Bellamystraat 8, 1053 BL Amsterdam
020 6183113
www.bakkerijpaulannee.nl

5. WILDERNIS

This urban gardening shop is the place to go for those with a city garden, balcony or roof terrace. They have an almost infinite number of (pretty!) garden tools, seeds and plant pots. For those short on outdoor space, they also offer house plants, plant hangers, botanical prints, mushroom-growing kits and books. If you're not blessed with green fingers, you can attend a workshop to learn how to grow vegetables on your balcony or how to arrange flowers. The great thing is, you can have a cup of coffee or tea as well, letting the calming energy of this green oasis sink in. This is my go-to place for garden inspiration.

Bilderdijkstraat 165F, 1053 KP Amsterdam
020 7852517
www.wildernisamsterdam.nl

6. CREATIEVE GARAGE

Yris and Joris opened their drop-off shop in an old garage in one of the prettiest and seemingly undiscovered streets of Oud-West – a street filled with little old houses and cute front gardens. Their space is crammed full of unique handmade products, such as jewellery, bags, tin toys, paintings and artworks supplied by people who want to show their work, but aren't well-known enough to open a shop of their own. This is also a creative hot-spot, where people come to work or give painting lessons. Locals come in for a cappuccino at the homey bar.

Bellamystraat 91, 1053 BJ Amsterdam
06 19979967
www.decreatievegarage.wordpress.com

7. FILMHALLEN

This former tram depot, where Amsterdam's first electric trams were maintained, now houses a cinema. With its nine screens, it's one of the largest cinemas in Amsterdam. They mainly screen art-house and quality Hollywood films. You can also simply walk in for a drink at the bar or to admire the beautiful archway.

Hannie Dankbaar Passage 12, 1053 RT Amsterdam
020 8208122
www.filmhallen.nl

ZAAL 4 - 5 - 6 - 8 - 9
PARISIENZAAL →

KOOK 4 A 5
MIN IN RUIM
KOKEND WATER

WARM DE SAUS OP
IN EEN SCHAAL
BOVENOP DE PAN

TIM VAN GIJZEL AND MENNO KATTENWINKEL

The shelves at **TIM** and **MENNO'S** shop, Holy Ravioli, are heaving with homemade ravioli. After owner Tim failed to find good ravioli elsewhere, he and Menno took matters into their own hands. Literally! They handmake and sell the most surprising varieties: with prawns, salsify root and confit of duck. They also sell cooked ravioli and soups to take away. People come from all over the city to buy their fresh pasta.

8. HOLY RAVIOLI
Jan Pieter Heijestraat 88, 1053 GS Amsterdam
020 6818414
www.holyravioli.nl

'We love cycling through Amsterdam, especially in summer.'

HOW WOULD YOU DESCRIBE AMSTERDAM?

Amsterdam is a city with a lot of creative free spirits, where different cultures come together and live together. This is clearly visible on our street, where everybody works together.

WHAT'S IN YOUR SECRET ADDRESS BOOK?

If we tell you, we'll have to kill you... But OK, if we have to divulge something: restaurant Mappa in the Nes is a hidden gem with friendly service and cool kitchen staff.

WHERE DO YOU GO TO FIND INSPIRATION?

We head to one of the following: Kanen Bij Ten Kate, Kanen Bij De Campus or Kanen Bij De Kachel. These open-air restaurants started here in Oud-West, at the Ten Katemarkt. This is where you'll find people with great professional passion.

WHAT'S YOUR FAVOURITE AREA?

Actually, we think all areas are cool; in our eyes, every neighbourhood has something going for it. There are some amazingly nice places in the south-east and also the new west.

WHAT IS ABSOLUTELY NOT TO BE MISSED IN AMSTERDAM?

Cycling through the city in summer.

9. JAN SCHILDER

Jan Schilder and his herring cart have been on the Bilderdijkstraat for years. It's an open secret that this is the place to go to for delicious herring. They sell like hot cakes. The fish are cleaned carefully and with love, each order prepared separately, taking a little time. This explains the long queue that usually snakes away from the cart. Don't be put off though, it's worth the wait.

Bilderdijkstraat (opposite Kwakersplein), Amsterdam

10. LAB 111

This place for filmmakers and film fans is hidden in the Helmersbuurt. It screens animated films as well as cinematographic documentaries and unconventional self-produced films. Lab 111 is housed in a former pathology lab and is very spacious. It's also a place where you can simply eat, and in the back there's an extraordinary garden with allotments and bee hives. Creative souls and art students flock to this hidden gem.

Arie Biemondstraat 111, 1054 PD Amsterdam
020 6169994
www.lab111.nl

11. DE FIETSKANTINE

This is Amsterdam's first bike repair shop, coffee bar and hairdresser in one. It's a cool hangout where you can have your bike fixed while drinking a cappuccino (at Lot Sixty One) or having a haircut (at Bubblekid) while you sit at the large table, surrounded by newspaper-reading locals. If you want to do some actual work, you can sit upstairs where there's a communal working space for freelancers. You'll always find something fun happening here.

Overtoom 141, 1054 HG Amsterdam
06 16365494
www.defietskantine.nl

12. FRIDAY NEXT

In this café/shop/interior design studio, you can sit anywhere you like and drink a smoothie or coffee. Locals come here with their laptops to work, to have business meetings or simply to eat a sandwich or salad. Everything's all jumbled up in this store, creating a nice, warm atmosphere. Their extraordinary offerings include fashion and interior design items by big brands, as well as exclusive products by Dutch designers. Check out their blog, too.

Overtoom 31, 1054 HB Amsterdam
020 6123292
www.fridaynext.com

13. KOFFIE ACADEMIE

A lot of local people come here for their first latte of the morning. Owner Jeffery roasts the coffee beans himself and the croissants and the carrot cake (both highly recommended!) are homemade. The raw vintage-style furniture, with lots of wood, designed by the owner himself, is for sale as is the ever-changing art by emerging artists.

Overtoom 95, 1054 HD Amsterdam
020 3707981
www.koffie-academie.nl

KOFFIE ACADEMIE

IT'S AMAZING HOW
A CUP OF GOOD
COFFEE CAN CHANGE
COFFEE YOUR DAY !

COFFEE + CROISSANT
€ 4.00
COFFEE + CAKE
€ 4.50

SHOPPING

2 DE BALKONIE
3 RASALILA D.I.Y. ATELIER
4 ACCESS TO TOOLS
6 THINGS I LIKE THINGS I LOVE
8 DE NIEUWE BOEKHANDEL

EATING & DRINKING

1 WHITE LABEL COFFEE

SLEEPING

5 HOTEL NOT HOTEL

MARKETS

7 ROMMELIGE ZONDAG

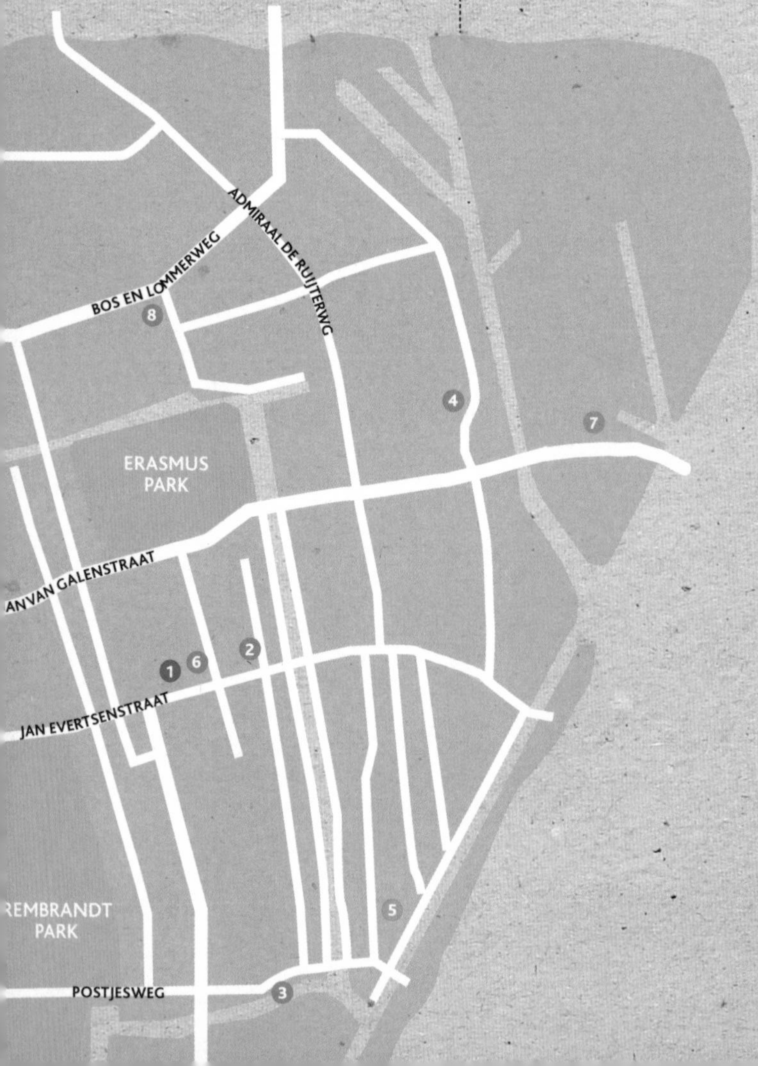

ADMIRAAL DE RUIJTERWG
BOS EN LOMMERWEG
8
4
7
ERASMUS PARK
ANVAN GALENSTRAAT
2
1
6
JAN EVERTSENSTRAAT
5
EMBRANDT PARK
POSTJESWEG
3

DE BAARSJES & BOS EN LOMMER

Until recently, declaring you were moving to one of these neighbourhoods would result in pitying looks. But these days, both areas are up-and-coming. De Baarsjes and Bos en Lommer are multicultural neighbourhoods with lots of young people and even more creativity. The large and busy 'Jan Eef' (the Jan Evertsenstraat) is home to some inspiring shops and coffee bars. You're in for a bit of a trek though, as they are few and far between. In Bos en Lommer (commonly referred to as 'Bolo') things are changing too, due to the arrival of artists and young families. Around the corner, on the Jan van Galenstraat, you'll find an extraordinary organic farm shop situated among the high-rise buildings. It's worth a visit.

1. WHITE LABEL COFFEE

If you like fuss-free coffee, then this coffee bar/
work space is the place for you. Owners Elmer
and Francesco are true coffee lovers, valuing its
pure flavour (they'd rather not add any milk or
favoured syrups). They source their beans from
Ethiopia and Sumatra and roast them out back,
behind the bar. You can also buy the beans to
take home. There's a changing art exhibition by
young designers and illustrators on the big wall.

Jan Evertsenstraat 136, 1056 EK Amsterdam
020 7371359
www.whitelabelcoffee.nl

2. DE BALKONIE

Friederike's shop is an endless source of inspiration for anyone with a balcony. Stocking plants and herbs that grow well in small shady spaces, as well as outdoor furniture, she also sells bird feeders, rugs and fake crows to scare away any pesky pigeons. Friederike confesses to not having a green thumb, but she sure does know how to make your balcony a nice place to be. Let her help you to transform your dull outdoor space into a cool hotspot.

**Jan Evertsenstraat 90, 1056 EG Amsterdam
06 28710318
www.debalkonie.nl**

3. RASALILA D.I.Y. ATELIER

This quirky shop, owned by sisters Floortje and Willemijn, is a paradise for fans of craft, sewing, paper art and fashion. It's an infinite source of DIY books, thread, paper, buttons, stamps and ribbons. At the back of the shop, around the large table, the sisters hold workshops in pattern drawing, interior styling, lip balm or cupcake making.

Postjesweg 15, 1057 DT Amsterdam
06 46390468
www.rasalila-atelier.nl

KLEUR
BOEKEN

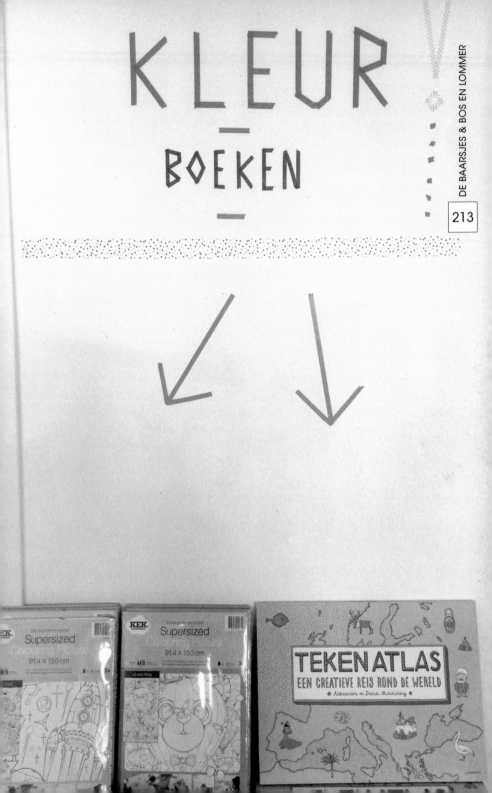

4. ACCESS TO TOOLS

This organic greengrocer sells vegetables, fruit and herbs freshly harvested from the city patch behind the shop. Natascha, the brains behind this initiative, and other locals are growing sustainable produce in the large courtyard, surrounded by high-rise buildings. Natascha is also trying to set up a food waste recycling unit. You can attend workshops here on things like how to to pickle fruit and veg. This is Natascha's way of contributing towards a more sustainable society.

Jasper Leijnsenstraat 21, 1056 XW Amsterdam
06 44504974
www.icanchangetheworldwithmytwohands.nl

5. HOTEL NOT HOTEL

This hotel, actually not a hotel, is directly opposite the large Westermoskee mosque (which is hard to miss). Created by a number of young designers (Collaboration-O) who met at the Design Academy Eindhoven, guests sleep in an old tram or a secret room behind a bookcase. Only a few rooms come with an en-suite bathroom, and a large living room is at the heart of it all. No wonder the place is filled with locals reading their papers, having lunch or drinking coffee.

Piri Reisplein 34, 1057 KH Amsterdam
020 8204538
www.hotelnothotel.com

SANNE OVERMAAT AND PETRA VERWAAL

On the border of the De Baarsjes and Bos en Lommer neighbourhoods, **SANNE** and **PETRA** run their concept store, Things I Like. Things I Love. Fine vintage and second-hand products, are displayed alongside clothes by emerging designers and their own label of beautiful basics. They only stock things that make their hearts beat faster. Sanne and Petra are hoping to bring inspiration to others, which is why everything they stock has been made with love and attention.

6. THINGS I LIKE THINGS I LOVE
Jan Evertsenstraat 106, 1056 EH Amsterdam
020 7894344
www.thingsilikethingsilove.nl

'Amsterdam is distinct, anonymous and free. A city where you can be yourself.'

HOW WOULD YOU DESCRIBE THE 'AMSTERDAM STYLE'?

Distinct, anonymous and free. A city where we can be ourselves, inspire each other and leave each other be at the same time.

WHAT'S IN YOUR SECRET ADDRESS BOOK?

Mana Mana, a fantastic Israeli place in the middle of De Pijp serving delicious bites. To catch a few rays of sunshine, we head to the terrace at Pacific for a beer – there's always a table available. The atmosphere is relaxed and, for a change, it's the opposite of hip.

WHERE DO YOU GO TO FIND INSPIRATION?

To SPRMRKT on the Rozengracht, the most beautiful and most creative shop in the city.

WHAT'S YOUR FAVOURITE AREA?

West, including the upcoming area of De Baarsjes. There's a lot to be experienced and discovered here. De Pijp has been changing for the better too these last few years. The yuppies have disappeared into the background and more and more lovely shops are opening. Both the Gerard Doustraat and the Ceintuurbaan are developing at a staggering speed.

WHAT'S STILL ON YOUR TO-DO LIST?
The Rijksmuseum is a must now that is has been renovated. It's the enormous queue of tourists that keeps putting us off.

WHAT IS ABSOLUTELY NOT TO BE MISSED IN AMSTERDAM?
The many food events and food markets. Every weekend without fail there's something foodie going on somewhere. The quality of food sold from food trucks is so good that it puts the most established restaurants in their place.

7. ROMMELIGE ZONDAG

Lovers of all things vintage will adore the (almost) monthly Rommelige Zondag (meaning 'messy Sunday') market in the Marktkantine, the former staff canteen of the Food Centre. Here, you can find really beautiful vintage pieces, second-hand designer clothes, retro goodies and up-cycled furniture. You can also sell your own wares. The difference between this market and your average flea market? Here you can drink great coffee too, eat a salad or stay on after the stalls close at 6 pm to listen to the DJs play their sets.

De Marktkantine
Jan van Galenstraat 6, 1051 KM Amsterdam
020 7231760
www.marktkantine.nl

8. DE NIEUWE BOEKHANDEL

Monique's bookshop is a much-loved place where book lovers meet. Here you'll find a wealth of surprising literature, cookbooks, children's books and e-readers on offer. The owner is an avid social media user who gives book-writing advice on Youtube. Writers come here to give lectures and once every three weeks, one book lover gets to spend the night in the shop. This idea originated from a Twitter post where a customer tweeted that he was locked inside a London book store and wanted to get out.

**Bos en Lommerweg 227, 1055 DT Amsterdam
020 4867722
www.denieuweboekhandel.nl**

OVERTOOM

VAN BAERLESTRAAT

VONDELPARK

③

WILLEMSPARKWEG

④

② ①

AMSTELVEENSEWEG

KONINGINNEWEG

DE LAIRESSESTRAAT

APOLLOLAAN

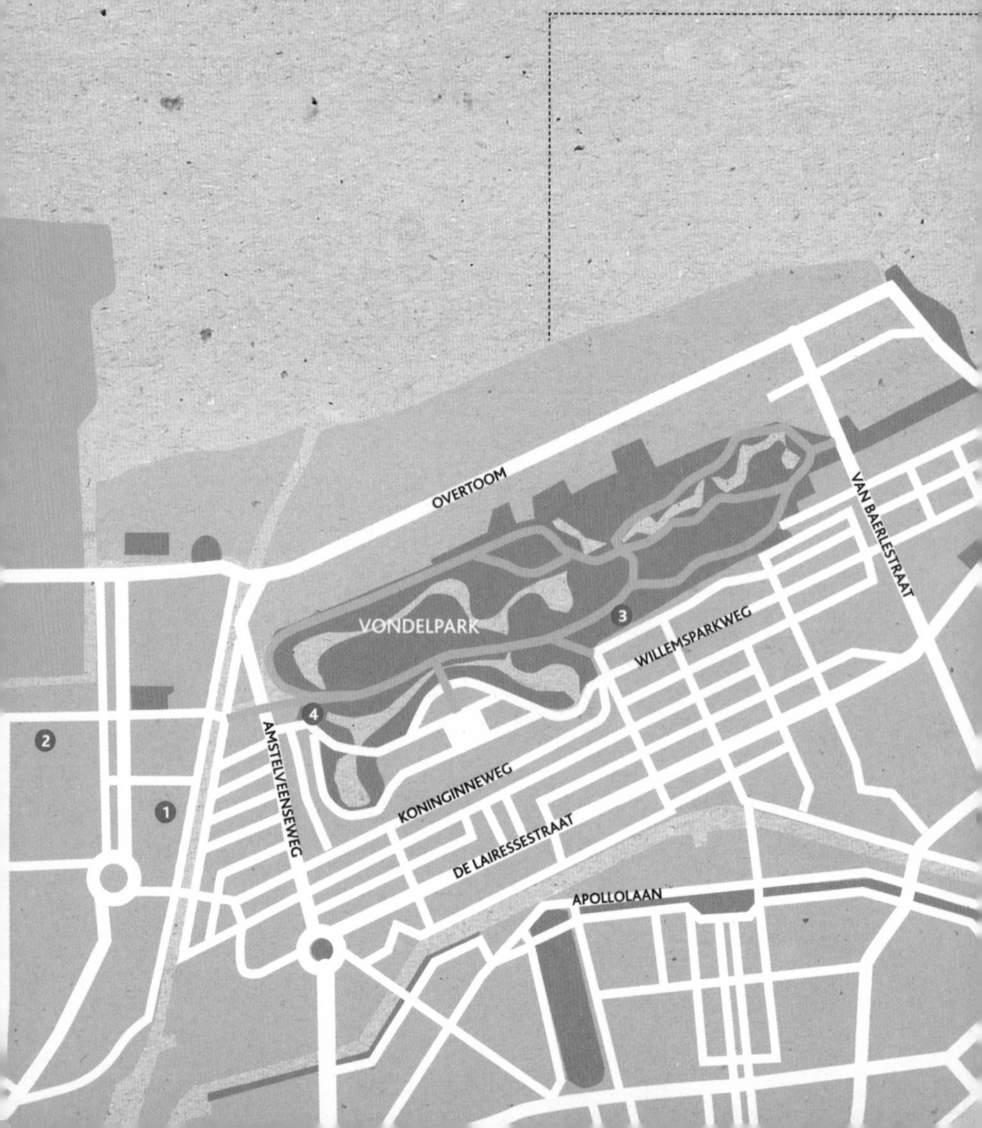

OUD-ZUID

Oud-Zuid (Old South) is one of the poshest areas in Amsterdam, especially the lush green streets surrounding the Concertgebouw, Museumplein and Vondelpark. The pretty green lanes, stately townhouses and the short distance to the city centre make it a favourite neighbourhood for celebrities and the rich. This area has many chic shops and well-known museums. To find the smaller, more extraordinary shops and lunch spots, head to the other side of Vondelpark and the Schinkelbuurt area.

1. VAN MECHELEN

This is an old-fashioned city café, but it's housed in a large industrial building with high ceilings and unfinished walls. This type of establishment is unusual for the area, making it all the more fun. The menu is classic yet relaxed (nice for a change) and boasts Belgian beers, bitterballen (a typical Dutch bar snack), cold cuts of meat and good cheeses. You can sit on a barstool at the counter and pretend you've stepped back in time, into a good old local pub.

Sloterkade 96–97, 1058 HK Amsterdam
020 2212348
www.stadscafevanmechelen.nl

2. CAFFÈNATION

Barista Bert is from Antwerp in Belgium and making the best coffee is his goal in life. He likes to keep things friendly and this shows: he's turned this coffee shop into a cosy living room. He roasts his own coffee beans, makes his own chocolate and serves hot cocoa made with real melted chocolate. Caffènation is a taste of Antwerp in Amsterdam. Even the furniture and art are made by Antwerp artists.

Theophile de Bockstraat 37i, 1058 TX Amsterdam
facebook.com/caffenationAmsterdam

MARJOLEIN VAN DER WAL

In her trademark Piaggio Ape, **MARJOLEIN** drives all over the city selling her super-healthy smoothies and juices. She is a self-confessed health freak and makes everything she sells herself using organic fruits and vegetables juiced in a slow-juicer, to keep all the nutrients in. You'll regularly find her in the area surrounding Vondelpark, and at festivals and small markets around town.

3. DE SAPKAR
06 28274869
www.de-sapkar.nl

'It is always
buzzing in the city
and something
exciting is about
to happen on
every street corner.'

HOW WOULD YOU DESCRIBE AMSTERDAM?

A city that is always buzzing, where something exciting is about to happen on every street corner. It's also a city where passionate people get a chance to do their thing.

WHAT'S IN YOUR SECRET ADDRESS BOOK?

Boekalicious, a lunch room-cum-cookery bookshop in Watergraafsmeer, serving organic croissants, delicious coffee and selling the prettiest cookbooks and culinary novels.

WHERE DO YOU GO TO FIND INSPIRATION?

To the Foodhallen and artisan markets such as NeighbourFood Market, Pure Markt and Sunday Market. This is where you find true professionals at work. They've taught me how to create a good look and vibe.

WHAT'S YOUR FAVOURITE AREA?

The Javastraat, where I live, is constantly developing, with new shops and coffee bars opening all the time.

WHAT'S STILL ON YOUR TO-DO LIST?
Definitely the Stedelijk Museum and the
Anne Frank House.

**WHAT IS ABSOLUTELY NOT TO BE
MISSED IN AMSTERDAM?**
Rollende Keukens (meaning 'rolling kitchens'),
a truck food festival held once a year in May,
and the NeighbourFood Market, a food market
held every third Sunday of the month, both at
the Westergasfabriek.

4. DE VONDELTUIN

This chill-out spot at the edge of Vondelpark is perfect for lazing about in a deckchair on the large sunny terrace. It almost feels like being in your own garden; no wonder locals treat it like their very own backyard. The atmosphere is bohemian (the pretty sixties pictures in the tiny café are a reminder of the flower power era). On Wednesday afternoons, the playground next door fills with children while their mums sip glasses of white wine nearby. Drinks are even allowed by the sandpit!

Vondelpark 7, 1075 VR Amsterdam
06 27565576
www.vondeltuin.nl

5. BLENDER

On the border of posh Oud-Zuid and hip De Pijp, Eline and Roelien (both mums of three) run their cosy family café – where you can have a sandwich or do some shopping. On Wednesday afternoons, a children's hairdresser drops by. Here, babies simply crawl on the floor and you don't have worry about spilling your glass of lemonade. On weekdays, the place is filled with yummy mummies and nannies with small kids. No wonder, there aren't many places like this one in the city.

Ruysdaelstraat 9–13, 1071 WX Amsterdam
020 8452615
www.blenderamsterdam.nl

Ombar €2.50
- Acai & Blueberry
- Goji Berry
- Dark 72%
- Lemon & Green Tea
- Coconut 60%
- Coconut 60%
- Coco Mi

235

6. TARWEGRASKONING

At Tarwegraskoning (which means 'wheatgrass king'), former yoga teacher and owner Auke sells all things wheatgrass. This is where Amsterdam's clean-living set come to order their personal stocks of fresh wheatgrass and sip on wheatgrass shots or smoothies at the window counter. For novices, Auke offers a milder carrot and beet shot. He also stocks a wide selection of superfoods, from hemp seed and physalis to spirulina and dark Chocodelic chocolate.

Roelof Hartstraat 10, 1071 VH Amsterdam
020 8200376
www.tarwegraskoning.nl

HET IJ

TRANSFORMATOR WEG

HOUT
HAVENS

1

7

WESTERGASFABRIEK

6 8 9   2

HAARLEMMERWEG

3

VAN HALLSTRAAT

NASSAUKADE

4

5

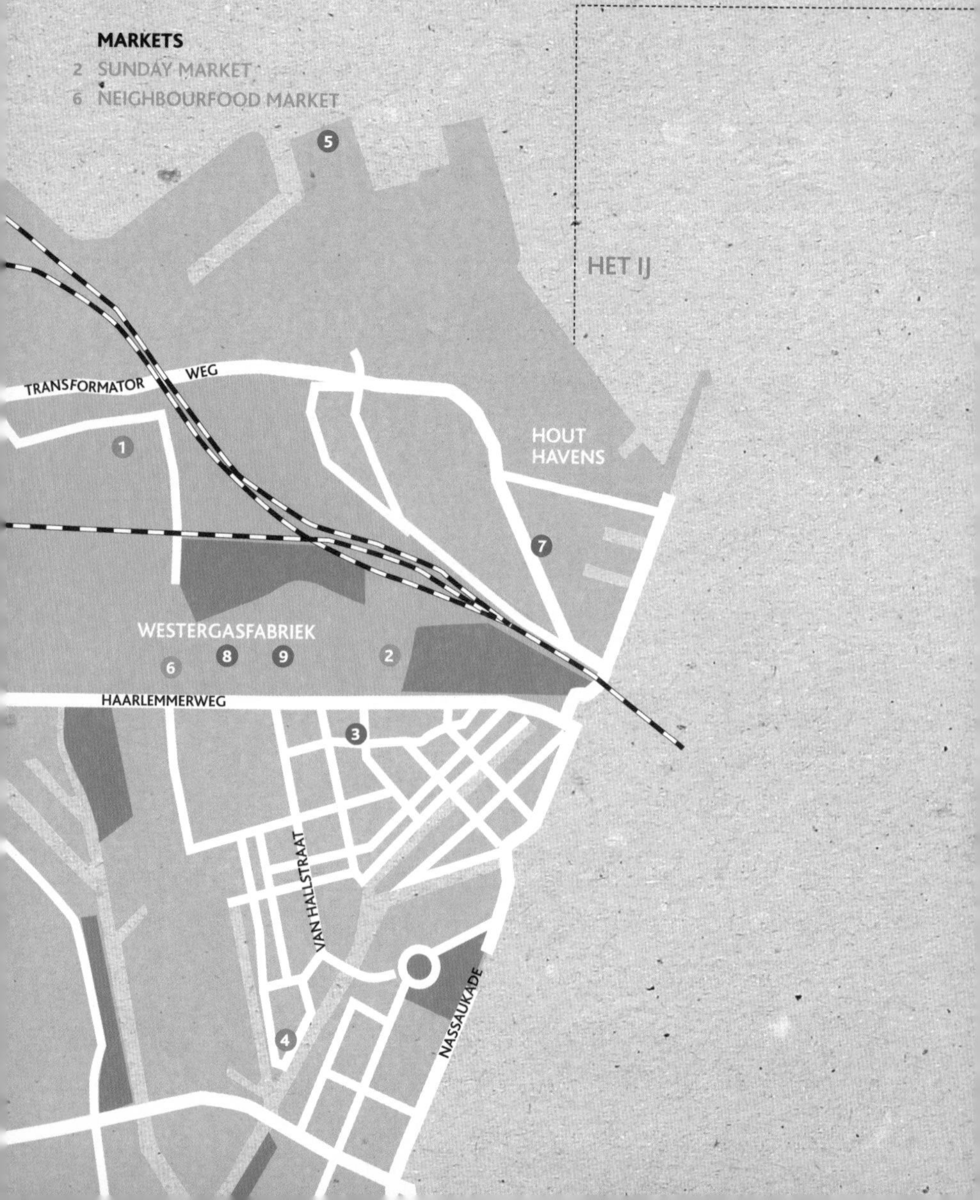

WESTERPARK

Westerpark is home to the former Westergasfabriek (Western Gas Factory) and this neighbourhood used to be a working-class area. In the sixties, the Staatsliedenbuurt became a mainstay for squatters. After extensive renovations, the area now houses a mix of different cultures, artists, families and students. The creative culture park Westerpark regularly hosts food and vintage markets, small festivals and temporary exhibitions. The more interesting places are to be found in the streets surrounding the park and across the railroad tracks in the Spaarndammerbuurt area. Many Amsterdam residents cycle quite a long way through the city to come here.

1. BUURTBOERDERIJ ONS GENOEGEN

When you're at this century-old neighbourhood farm, you'll feel at one with nature even though you're in the middle of the city. Sheep, chickens and goats roam freely and the grounds are full of beautiful flowers and medicinal herbs. There's food and drink to be had, and you can attend a concert or yoga class, or watch a film at the open-air cinema. It's run entirely by volunteers. Do pop into the Weggeefwinkel (meaning 'give-away shop') where used products get a new lease of life, in true Mahatma Gandhi spirit: 'The world has enough for everyone's needs, but not everyone's greed.'

Spaarndammerdijk 319, 1014 AA Amsterdam
020 3376820
www.buurtboerderij.nl

2. SUNDAY MARKET

This monthly market held on the grounds of the former Westergasfabriek (Western Gas Factory) was inspired by London's Spitalfields and Camden markets. Here you can shop, eat, find inspiration and have fun on the merry-go-round. You'll find lots of vintage clothing, retro gear, handmade ceramics, jewellery, art and pretty things made by emerging designers. The atmosphere is relaxed and there are children running around the stalls. As the market is only held one Sunday a month, it's best to check the website before you go.

Haarlemmerweg 8–10, 1014 BE Amsterdam
www.sundaymarket.nl

3. DE CULINAIRE WERKPLAATS

Design duo Marjolein and Eric create food concepts that inspire people to consume more consciously. Their ideas follow themes such as 'red', 'flowers' or 'emotions', and they design dishes accordingly. They mainly work for other companies, but on Fridays and Saturdays, you can visit their restaurant. On these nights, Marjolein and Eric cook five surprising dishes based on their monthly theme.

Fannius Scholtenstraat 10, 1051 EX Amsterdam
06 54646576
www.deculinairewerkplaats.nl

ANNEMIEKE BOOTS

Artist **ANNEMIEKE** makes beautiful crockery, bowls, spoons and other ceramic objects that shine in their simplicity and fragility. Her cosy workshop on the water's edge exudes a serene calm. You can watch her at work nearly every day of the week, working on a wheel or by hand. She uses gres and porcelain clay, forever on the lookout for new ways to use these materials. Annemieke enjoys working with the elements of earth, water and fire and this joy shows in her work. Annemieke, who shares her workshop with artists Marie-José Schulte and Bill William, also sells her pottery to restaurants and shops.

4. ANNEMIEKE BOOTS CERAMICS
Buyskade 128, 1051 ME Amsterdam
www.annemiekebootsceramics.nl

'I love the freedom
and creativity of
this city, where
everyone gets to
be who they are.'

WHAT DOES AMSTERDAM MEAN TO YOU?

Amsterdam, to me, is freedom, creativity and possibility. Everyone gets to be who they are. The city is small and large at the same time. Small, because you can cover most of it by bike or on foot. Large, because of the diversity in cultures and styles. I don't think there is a specific Amsterdam style – anything goes!

WHAT'S IN YOUR SECRET ADDRESS BOOK?

Outras Coisas in De Jordaan is a small shop with lovely home accessories, clothes and jewellery. The owner is nice to chat to and you'll discover a pretty bowl, bag or candle in every nook and cranny.

WHERE DO YOU GO TO FIND INSPIRATION?

I go and have coffee in a coffee shop or concept store, to share ideas with a friend or design a new pottery line in a nice environment. Favourites are Cottoncake in De Pijp, but also Coffee & Juices at Hugo de Grootplein and KOKO Coffee & Design in the city centre.

WHAT ARE YOUR FAVOURITE AREAS?

De Jordaan and Oud-West. I live in Oud-West with its huge variety of shops, coffee bars, Vondelpark, the Ten Katemarkt and all kinds of restaurants. De Jordaan however has its own unique atmosphere, with its canals and the Haarlemmerstraat, home store Aarde on the Westerstraat, natural drugstore Lavendula and, around the corner, the farmers' market on Saturdays.

WHAT'S STILL ON YOUR TO-DO LIST?

There are several parks still on my wish list. I'd like to have a look at Park Frankendael in the Watergraafsmeer area. Once a month, it hosts the Pure Markt with its regional and artisan food. It'll be nice to combine the two.

5. DOK

The inhabitants of Amsterdam love a good beach bar. You can feel the wind in your hair and sit by the water without ever having to leave the city. At Dok, the atmosphere is laid back; they light bonfires and you can have a glass of wine or do some yoga. Children can play around the containers without being disturbed. On sunny days, it's a great place to lounge in a deck chair with a view of the IJ, and you can stay way beyond sunset. Mind you, you cannot swim here.

Moermanskkade 71, 1013 BC Amsterdam
06 19860087
www.dokamsterdam.nl

6. NEIGHBOURFOOD MARKET

If food that is grown and produced with love and care is your thing, you'd better not miss this market held on the grounds of the Westergasfabriek. On the third Sunday of each month, local farmers, juicers, soup makers, tea and beer brewers, cheese and sausage makers set up their organic shops here. It's a wonderful place to browse the stalls or enjoy a meal with friends at one of the long trestle tables. Don't forget to check out the bric-a-brac, second-hand and vintage product section next door. The atmosphere is always relaxed, making this a lovely place to spend a sunny Sunday.

**Polonceaukade 27, 1014 DA Amsterdam
www.neighbourfood.nl**

7. DOPHERT

Vegans can eat here to their heart's content. Laura and Balda opened their restaurant, the first fully vegan lunch spot (egg and lactose free) in Amsterdam, in the up-and-coming Spaarndammerstraat. They serve toasties with seitan (wheat gluten) chorizo, almond milk, scrambled tofu and pumpkin hummus, and lots of delicious homemade pies. Upstairs, you'll find tables and colourful chairs and walls covered in changing artworks. Not a hippie in sight.

Spaarndammerstraat 49, 1013 ST Amsterdam
020 7520581
www.dophertcatering.nl

8. MOSSEL & GIN

If you're looking for a place with a little bit of that New York feel, look no further. Owners Josh and Wouter have taken up residence in the cutest little building on the grounds of the Westergasfabriek for their seafood bar. Their offerings are sure to widen your culinary horizons — you'll be surprised how many variations on the theme are possible. The interior decoration is no-nonsense and the limited number of tables make it a very cosy place. In summer, the enormous terrace is wonderful, too. To be enjoyed with a gin and tonic, as the name suggests.

Gosschalklaan 12, 1014 DC Amsterdam
020 4865869
www.mosselengin.nl

WE ZIJN EEN BE
BEVOOROORDEELD. M
BIJ PREMIER DENKEN
DAT MOSSELEN HET
ALLERLEKKERSTE ETEN IS
DAT ER BESTAAT. EN WAT
JE MISSCHIEN NIET WIST,
MOSSELEN ZIJN OOK NOG
EENS HEEL GEZOND. ZE
BEVATTEN WEINIG VET,
AAR DES TE MEER
WITTEN, MINERALEN,
. FOSFOR EN
INEN EN HET BEETJE
AT ER IN ZIT IS OOK
NS GEZOND VET.

carrot cake

Coo kie
- chocola
oatmeal
noten

SLOW COFFEES:

v60 ↓ 3.40

aeropress ↓ 3.40

chemex ↘
(to share) ↙
6.00

WESTERPARK

253

9. ESPRESSOFABRIEK

This relaxed coffee bar is hidden between the many industrial buildings on the grounds of the former Westergasfabriek. Owner Rik roasts the coffee beans in his attic – look up and you'll see sacks of them lying about. On weekdays the place is full of freelancers tapping on their laptops and settling in for the afternoon. They serve authentic old-fashioned apple pie to go with the delicious coffee.

Pazzanistraat 39, 1014 DB Amsterdam
020 4862106
www.espressofabriek.nl

5 JAVA-EILAND

IJ HAVEN

1 2 KNSM LAAN
3 KNSM-EILAND

PIET HEINKADE

OOSTELIJKE HANDELSKADE 4

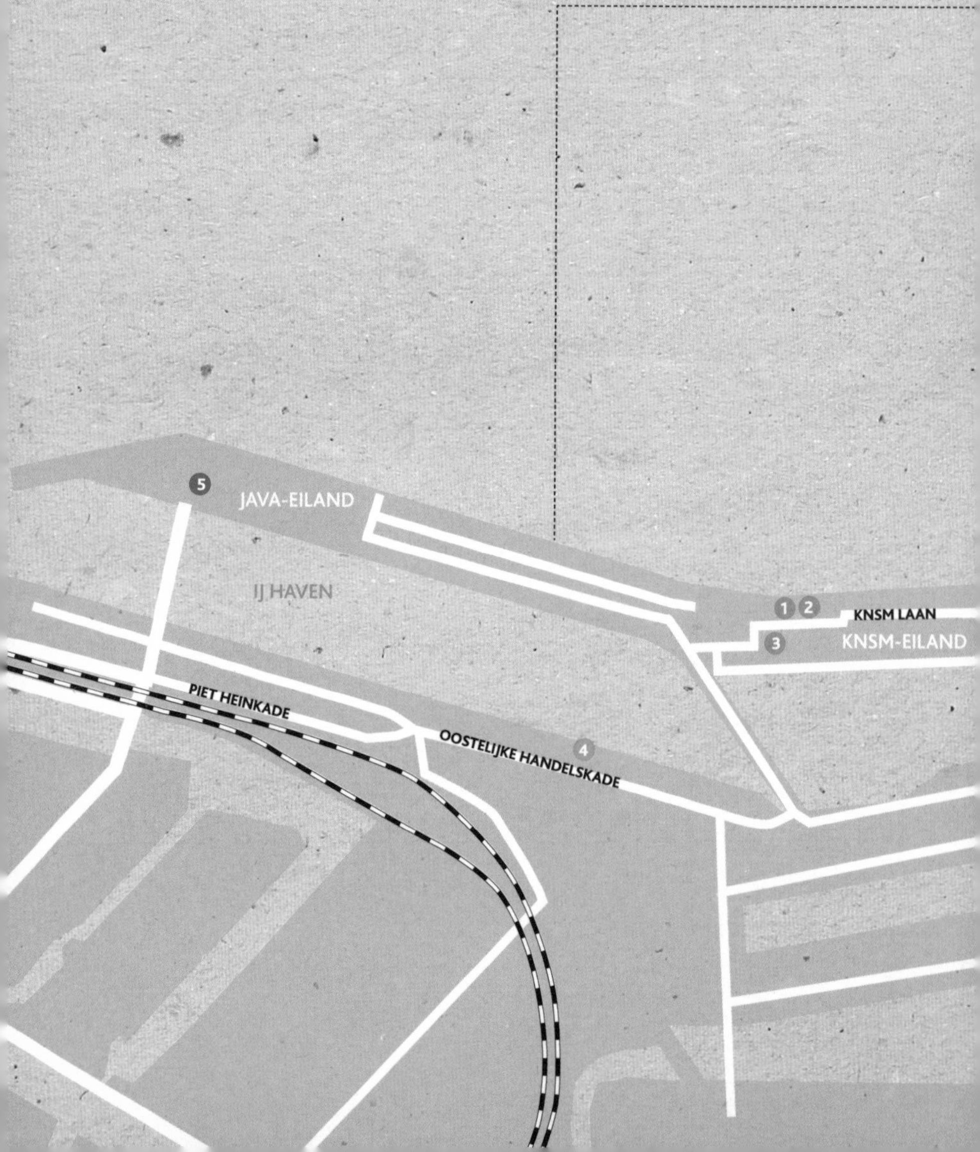

OOSTELIJK HAVENGEBIED

The Oostelijk Havengebied (Eastern Docklands) is a must for lovers of modern architecture. The city's docks were once located here; later it became a place where artists and squatters settled. The old wharf buildings and the high quays remain unchanged and make for an interesting contrast with the more recently constructed residential buildings. The Oostelijk Havengebied consists of a few islands, including KNSM and Java; the former named after the Royal Dutch Steamboat Shipping company (Koninklijke Nederlandse Stoomboot-Maatschappij), which was originally based there. The area has a unique atmosphere: metropolitan and village-like at the same time. It's a great area for strolling around, gazing out over the IJ and wandering into the little shops situated in the old warehouses and wharf buildings.

1. SISSY-BOY

I can spend hours perusing shops like these. Sissy-Boy sells pretty fashion items (for kids as well as adults) and beautiful home accessories such as vases, crockery, robust bowls, pretty throws, notebooks, paper and nicely designed books. I get new ideas and inspiration every time I visit. The house blend coffee in the shop café is tasty and there is plenty to look at while you're sitting. To find even more inspiration, go to Pols Potten next door (see page 258).

KNSM-laan 19, 1019 LA Amsterdam
020 4191559
See www.sissy-boy.com for more locations

LUCAS PRIESMAN

If you like Dutch design, head to the beautiful KNSM Island. In one of the former warehouses you'll find Pols Potten, a shop crammed full of vases, lamps, crockery, tables, sofas, textiles and beautiful books from their own designers as well as others. The team behind this shop works with young talent, who get the opportunity to exhibit their collections in the back of the warehouse. Sometimes, these items are included in the shop's stock. Need more advice on living and styling? Head to neighbouring Sissy-Boy (see page 257).

2. POLS POTTEN
KNSM-laan 39, 1019 LA Amsterdam
020 4193541
www.polspotten.nl

'Amsterdam is like
a warm blanket.
It is worldly, but
as a metropolis
it's quite small.'

HOW WOULD YOU DESCRIBE AMSTERDAM?

Amsterdam is worldly, but as a metropolis it's quite small. I love this city because it has everything: all kinds of art, architecture, fashion, advertisers, design and a mixed population. Amsterdam is like a warm blanket. I feel secure here: I understand the code and speak the language.

WHAT'S IN YOUR SECRET ADDRESS BOOK?

Before I open up the shop in the morning I pop in to Helena Primakoff on the Czaar Peterstraat for a crunchy muesli with yoghurt, a fresh juice and a cortado.

WHERE DO YOU GO TO FIND INSPIRATION?

The Stedelijk Museum, where past and present come together beautifully. Beauty and ugliness meet there and at the point at which they meet, I find inspiration. And I also find it when I ride my bike in the rural Noord area.

WHAT'S YOUR FAVOURITE AREA?

De Pijp. For the longest time, I thought this neighbourhood was overrated; that it thought it was the be-all and end-all. But this area has snuck back into my good graces lately – it's nice and lively.

WHAT IS ABSOLUTELY NOT TO BE MISSED IN AMSTERDAM?

The Dappermarkt in the eastern part of town at 9 am when the stands are being divided up. The voices, the dialects, the havoc caused, but most of all, the smiley Mokummers (as inhabitants of Amsterdam call themselves) you find there. A good laugh.

3. ART & FLOWERS

This tiny atelier is filled to the brim with beautiful flowers and vases. Co-owners Eduard and Marcellus are masters of combining flowers and art – they make the prettiest creations. They're always on the lookout for the latest trends and they design arrangements for events and special occasions. They do extraordinary bouquets too.

KNSM-laan 6, 1019 LL Amsterdam
020 4192273
www.artandflowers.nl

4. LLOYD HOTEL

Looking around the dizzyingly high living room of this Amsterdamse School-style stately building, you could almost forget you're in a hotel. Many people come here for business lunches or coffee, and in summer, the large, sunny terrace at the back is great for relaxing. More than fifty artists collaborated on the interior of the hotel, creating a unique design for each room. In the past, the building had several other uses: the shipping company Koninklijke Hollandsche Lloyd (meaning 'Royal Dutch Lloyd') built the hotel, and after they went bankrupt in 1935, the building became a refugee centre, a detention centre and, later, artists' studios.

Oostelijke Handelskade 34, 1019 BN Amsterdam
020 5613636
www.lloydhotelamsterdam.nl

265

5. JAVA BLEND

Robert was one of the first inhabitants of Java island and he used to dream of having a large living-room style space where locals, tourists and freelancers could meet. One look inside his coffee house reveals him to be an interior stylist. Fully decorated in twenties Art Deco style, his café is a nod to the peak years of the former eastern docklands and the island's warehouses. Downstairs, you'll find a free little library where you can swap books, and there's always art from Robert's fellow islanders on display.

Tosaristraat 1, 1019 RT Amsterdam
020 3585225
www.javablendamsterdam.nl

ABOUT THE AUTHOR

MONIQUE VAN DEN HEUVEL is a lifestyle journalist and social media specialist. She has worked for Dutch lifestyle magazines such as *Happinez* and *Flow*. She's been living in Amsterdam for over twenty years and is always on the lookout for extraordinary and original places to inspire her work and her life. Monique believes creativity is the key to success. For this book, she has gone in search of stylish little shops, coffee bars and other special places with a story to tell – places where the owners and staff love what they do. Monique likes vintage, flowers, art and craftsmanship and she's passionate about all things handmade, natural and organic. In this book, she shares more than 100 of her favourite Amsterdam spots.

INDEX

Published in 2016 by Murdoch Books, an imprint of Allen & Unwin
First published in Holland in 2015 by Kosmos Uitgevers, Utrecht/Antwerpen

Murdoch Books Australia
83 Alexander Street
Crows Nest NSW 2065
Phone: +61 (0) 2 8425 0100
Fax: +61 (0) 2 9906 2218
murdochbooks.com.au
info@murdochbooks.com.au

Murdoch Books UK
Ormond House
26–27 Boswell Street
London WC1N 3JZ
Phone: +44 (0) 20 8785 5995
murdochbooks.co.uk
info@murdochbooks.co.uk

For Corporate Orders & Custom Publishing, contact our Business Development Team
at salesenquiries@murdochbooks.com.au

Publisher: Corinne Roberts
Translator: Suzanne Stougie
Designer: Femke den Hertog
Cover design: Sarah Odgers © Murdoch Books 2016

Text and photography (excluding below) © Monique van den Heuvel 2015
Additional photography: p. 8 Niels Luigjes; p. 17, 18, 19 Jeltje Janmaat, SeenByBien; p. 58 Jitske Hagens
(Wij Zijn Kees); p. 100, 102, 103 SeenByBien; p. 122, 123 Chris van Houts; p. 124 Carolien Baudoin;
p. 135 Heleen Peeters, Lotte Klösters

A cataloguing-in-publication entry is available from the catalogue of the National Library of Australia
at nla.gov.au.

ISBN 978 1 74336 893 0 Australia
ISBN 978 1 74336 896 1 UK

A catalogue record for this book is available from the British Library.

Colour reproduction by Splitting Image Colour Studio Pty Ltd, Clayton, Victoria
Printed by 1010 Printing International Limited, China